M

# A Practical
# Church Administration
# Handbook

# A PRACTICAL
# CHURCH ADMINISTRATION
# HANDBOOK

by
Norman E. Nygaard

BAKER BOOK HOUSE
Grand Rapids 6, Michigan
1962

Library of Congress Catalog Card Number: 62–19236

PHOTOLITHOPRINTED BY CUSHING - MALLOY, INC.
ANN ARBOR, MICHIGAN, UNITED STATES OF AMERICA
1962

# PREFACE

All agree that the smooth operation of a church prepares the way for fruitful and pleasurable service. This book is a valuable aid toward the attainment of that goal.

This is a book of wide usefulness. It answers many questions and solves many problems which confront the average pastor and church member. One need only scan the Table of Contents to learn how it may be of help to those charged with responsibility in the program of the church.

Have you responsibility in the matter of publicizing your church? Does your church have an effective program for meeting strangers and integrating new members? How good and how complete is your church membership record? Could your church ushering be improved? These questions suggest just a few areas in which this book will prove helpful.

This book was prepared by one who for a number of years devoted himself to giving counsel and guidance in the sphere of church administration. His advice was based not only on theory, but on years of practical experience in the active ministry.

This book should be purchased in quantities for distribution to all those who voluntarily and gladly give hours of devoted service in the work of and for the church.

The Publishers

# TABLE OF CONTENTS

# 1

## PROVEN METHODS FOR PUBLICIZING YOUR CHURCH

1. Newspaper Musts
2. Radio Publicity
3. The Cumulative Value of Publicity
4. Writing Your Church Notices
5. Newspaper Advertising
6. A Typical Church News Story

# PROVEN METHODS FOR PUBLICIZING YOUR CHURCH

Obtaining publicity for the church is not a difficult feat at all if you will bear in mind certain salient facts. I have frequently had Protestant ministers protest against the amount of publicity which is often accorded the Roman Catholic church and the small amount of publicity which they are able to obtain.

There is no conspiracy upon the part of the Fourth Estate to give undue space in their columns to any church, Protestant or Catholic, or Jewish synagogue. Many Protestant churches seem to have no difficulty whatsoever in getting their articles accepted BUT THEY ARE THE CHURCHES WHOSE PUBLICITY REPRESENTATIVES MAKE IT EASY FOR THE NEWSPAPERS TO PUBLISH THEIR ARTICLES.

## NEWSPAPER *MUSTS*

If you will bear in mind a few simple facts about the newspaper business you will see why some churches are regularly represented in the news columns of newspapers and why other churches are rarely there. These are the facts which we would call to your attention:

1. Newspaper men tell me that they are chronically lazy. Some few men in the game may be, but the fact is that most newspapermen work at top speed meeting impossible deadlines. They have had to learn to do their job as expeditiously and quickly as possible. When an article comes to the desk of the man who handles the church page — just as one of a number of assignments — and when that article is written in typical newspaper style so that all it needs is a heading he will take it in preference to some other article which is single-spaced or written by hand and which will need considerable revision. The first article will take up five minutes of that man's busy time. The second may require forty-five minutes to prepare for the paper. The first article gets published — no matter what denomination it represents. The second will be condensed to a paragraph if it is published at all.

2. News stories should be newsworthy. Anything that is different or out of the ordinary which can be played up in an article gives it vital content.

A great evangelist who was having trouble getting articles about his meetings published complained to me that an evangelist had to run off with a blonde to get into the paper. I took a look at the articles which he was handing in to the papers and told him that if he would spend fifteen minutes with me on a short course on article preparation I'd guarantee to get good newspaper coverage.

We took the articles which he intended to turn in, extracted some startling statements from them, and played them up in our lead sentence, and took them to the newspaper office. He met the church editor and we had a brief chat. I suggested that the newspaper photographer could get a wonderful crowd shot either in the auditorium or of people coming out and reminded the editor that crowds really were coming to the meetings. The man took the hint and we had a picture the next day of the multitude which attended that evening service. A day later we had another picture of the evangelist meeting some of the prominent people in the community. It is still true in the newspaper business that "when a man bites a dog it's news."

3. There is another very important principle to remember and it is this: Names make news. That is as true of the large metropolitan newspaper as of the small-town sheet. The difference is that in newspapers serving towns of less than 125,000 people *any* name is newsworthy. In the larger papers there should always be a sprinkling of well-known names in an article to get it printed. For instance if the Ladies' Aid Society of the First Baptist Church elects a slate of officers it is well to select a prominent name from the list and feature it even though the lady in question may be only the quilting chairman. The other names assume prominence because they are linked with hers.

You may object to that as undemocratic. We are mentioning it without comment as one of the facts of life with which we must be acquainted if we are to get the publicity that our church deserves.

4. Another important fact is this: you will get more and better publicity for your church if you will get acquainted with the church editor and will go out of your way to express your appreciation for the publicity which he is giving you. He will tell you that it is just a part of his job and that he deserves no credit for his work but just the same he will appreciate your word of appreciation — AND HE WILL REMEMBER YOU. He'll get your stories in if he can.

## RADIO PUBLICITY

Many churches are missing the boat because they are apparently still unaware of the fact that the news period on the radio is available to them if they have items which can be used.

Many radio stations announce different kinds of meetings. They are eager for news about clubs and organizations and will be glad to make anouncement about the doings of your men's clubs, your youth groups, your women's societies, if you will supply them with the information. You can 'phone in that information or send it in on a postal card.

If you have a prominent speaker — especially if he or she is dealing with some controversial subject — you can get considerable coverage from the radio station and occasionally even from the news broadcasts of your TV station.

You can also get time on a TV station for an interview with that person. If he has just spoken in your church let that fact be known. If he is to speak that fact should be played up. The important thing is to work in the name of your church.

## THE CUMULATIVE VALUE OF PUBLICITY

The public relations man for a mid-western university once told me that he wasn't afraid of adverse publicity or criticism. He said that he was always delighted when his school received favorable publicity but he would rather have criticisms of the school get into the newspapers than not to have the newspapers mention the institution at all.

His institution was a church college but he still felt that the important thing was to have the college mentioned — no matter in what connection.

I realize that conservative churchmen abhor any unfavorable publicity, but the fact is that publicity will build up church attendance. However, conservative churches, if they are so-minded, can take a series of sermons on the Ten Commandments and by shrewd publicity measures build them up so that people will be curious and will want to attend the services to hear what the minister has to say about covetousness, false witness, and the other sins which the commandments forbid.

## WRITING YOUR CHURCH NOTICES

In some newspapers there are regular church notices which are set up in a certain prescribed form. Church members and people who are looking around for a church home do read those notices. Every church invited to send in notices to those columns should never fail to do so.

However, on the church page there are also special articles, sometimes illustrated, which recount some special features — anniversaries, dedications, unique services, etc. It is not advisable to send in an article every week but certainly every legitimate occasion for an article should be utilized.

Following are a few special observations on the way to write such articles so that they will be considered for publication:

1. Don't try to put a heading on your article. This is the editor's job and even though you know how to write a heading don't do it.

2. Always leave the top third of a sheet of paper on which your news article is written with no writing whatsoever. If you want the article to go into a certain issue of the paper you can put a release date in the upper left-hand corner with some such notation as this — "Do not release until Feb. 28th." If this is done run as close to the top of the sheet as possible.

3. Always triple-space. The cardinal sin in newspaper writing is to single-space an article. The reason for triple-spacing, of course, is to allow editorial blue-penciling.

4. Always tell the entire story in your lead sentence. The material which follows is merely an elaboration of the lead. The lead sentence should capture the interest of the reader and make him want to go on and read the rest of the story. A typical lead sentence would be the following:

"Drug addiction is one of the greatest problems facing our military commanders of troops in the orient," declared the Rev. Dr. Mason Bligh, minister of the Copley Square Congregational Church of New York. "The Communists are making strenuous efforts to debauch American soldiers by introducing them to the drug habit."

Such a sentence would immediately command interest. The reader would want to go on and ascertain what more the minister would say.

The writer could then go on to give a further account of his activity, mentioning the fact that he had visited the troops at the invitation of such-and-such an organization and announce the place and time where the Rev. Mr. Bligh would be speaking.

5. Articles should always be written in the third person. The first person is used only on the editorial pages. Whenever the first person is used it should always be in quotation marks. A typical example follows: "I was never so surprised in all my life," the Rev. John Fellows exclaimed as the chairman of the Board of Trustees of the First Methodist Church, Mr. William McIntyre, handed over to him the keys to a new Pontiac, gift of the congregation on the occasion of the tenth anniversary of the beginning of his pastorate.

6. Newspaper articles preferably consist of three, five, or seven paragraphs. Longer articles can have any number of paragraphs. Most church articles, of course, will not be longer than five paragraphs unless they are reporting an unusual conference.

This is a newspaper device which is used primarily to give balance to the appearance of an article in print. A two paragraph article looks awkward. You can generally depend on being given at least three paragraphs if your article is to be used at all.

7. Editors must often cut articles to meet the needs of available space. A seven-paragraph article may be cut to five or three paragraphs. A five-paragraph article may be cut to three. Always be sure that if a cut is made the three paragraphs that did get in are complete in and of themselves.

## NEWSPAPER ADVERTISING

Most newspapers offer special rates to churches. Frankly, in small town newspapers there is very little point in purchasing advertising space when weekly articles on the church's activities are welcomed. In cities of from 75,000 to 150,000 population newspaper space is not particularly expensive and will make your church message stand out. In larger cities it is almost a must to buy space if you want to reach a city constituency.

Neighborhood churches will not need advertising space in the paper as much as downtown churches but it may be advisable to purchase it just to keep the church's name before the people.

The most effective advertisements are not those which give the name of the church, the announcement of the minister's theme and his name. Instead, they are the ads with homey little messages which tell something about the church.

The off-brand churches take considerable space and often feature an evangelist with an open Bible. They find it effective in attracting those who go to church to hear a sensational message concerning the impending doom of the world. They would not attract people who go to church to hear a constructive message related to the problems which they face in daily life, or words of comfort and guidance.

But homey, challenging short messages, possibly relating to the minister's theme the following Sunday, or just concerned with the answers that faith has to the day's pressing problems will arouse attention — and increase attendance.

It is wise to make brief announcement of the time of the service or services and a notation regarding the sermon theme but the basis of the advertisement is to give people something which will cause them to think.

Churches using this method would be wise to submit this weekly message to a professional advertising man to check with him on their effectiveness but they can be assured that such an ad will pull people to church — especially if theirs is the only church employing this device.

A small cut of the church, a distinctive cross, or some other format which is always employed as a trade-mark is valuable for this purpose.

## A TYPICAL CHURCH NEWS STORY

*We have set forth a typical news story. It should be typed and double spaced. Allow space at top for editor to write in the heading. If you will observe its form carefully you will find that the newspapers will gladly accept these from your church. It is merely an announcement of a special speaker, but it is written in the form which you should use in writing all your news stories.*

After thirty years spent in India where he served as principal of the Agricultural Institute at Allahabad, Dr. Samuel Higginbottam who is one of the world's leading authorities in the field of agriculture reported that it was possible to increase production thirty-fold on the small farms of India by using scientific methods. In his own work Dr. Higginbottam demonstrated this fact again and again.

Dr. Higginbottam was recently knighted by the queen of England and is presently serving as moderator of the Presbyterian Church in the United States of America, one of three laymen who in the one hundred and fifty years history of that denomination has been so honored. He will speak Sunday evening in the First Presbyterian Church at 7:30 o'clock. The church is located at the corner of First Avenue and Main Street.

The son of a Welsh coal-miner who emigrated to this country in order to enter the School of Agriculture at Cornell University, Dr. Higginbottam has had a most eventful career. He went to India as a missionary in 1904 and in the years that have followed has developed the little trade school to which he was sent into one of the great agricultural colleges of the world.

Dr. Higginbottam is spending his furlough year in visiting every synod of his denomination. The First Presbyterian Church was selected as the host church because of its large auditorium and the desire of church officials that Dr. Higginbottam should be able to reach the largest number of Presbyterian constitutents and people who are interested in foreign missions as possible.

Dr. Higginbottam has chosen as the theme for his message, "Foreign Missions On the March". "In all of the countries of Asia people are interested not only in improvements in agriculture, better schooling, and the establishment of hospitals and clinics but in the Gospel of Jesus Christ," Dr. Higgibottam stated. "There is a hunger for the message of salvation. Men and women everywhere in the Far East feel that Christianity is the only answer to the need of the world."

# 2

## HANDBOOK FOR CHURCH CALLING

# HANDBOOK FOR CHURCH CALLING

There is a special technique in church visitation, both in calling upon church members and also those who are prospects for church membership. Most church boards have long ago been liberated from the notion that calls should be made entirely by ministers. They realize that, although the minister presumably will want to do his share in this task, whether he is the minister of a large church or a small one, the business of church visitation should not be his alone. And if the minister can be released from routine visitation he can spend his time in calling upon people who have serious problems and, when the time is ripe, upon prospects for church membership.

In small churches the minister will naturally want to make an occasional call upon every member of his parish and will normally expect to do so. In a large church, particularly in the city, a minister will find it impossible to reach every member in his calling although very frequently his members will assume that it is his responsibility to do so.

## WHERE THE MINISTER IS MOST EFFECTIVE

Every minister will want to call upon people who are seriously ill and upon homes which have been bereft; and he will be asked to make such calls upon many who are not members of or associated with his church in any way. He will be called upon to help out in the case of family disputes, particularly difficulties between husbands and wives. These are calls where he can be of the greatest assistance but he cannot devote the time to such situations which he should handle if he is expected to "make the rounds" of his congregation.

He will probably be the person who will make the final call upon prospective church members but it will save his time if others call upon these people first to ascertain if they are really prospects for church membership or if they dropped in at the church because they arose too late to travel the distance to the church of which they were members, or if they were merely casual attendants on one particular Sunday.

## WHERE CHURCH MEMBERS CAN BE PARTICULARLY HELPFUL

If a church has a corps of visitors, many of them church officers or people who are active in other church activities, they can be of immense assistance to the minister and with their co-operation a very close-knit church membership can be formed and new members added in considerable number.

For routine church calling a city or community can be divided into districts with a certain number of callers responsible for each district. To them would be referred the names of people who had recently visited the church (preferably during the week after they attended) in addition to the regular calls which they would make upon the people who lived in their area.

In the diagram below we have divided a mythical city into districts to show how a calling committee is organized. Larger cities would have more divisions and sub-divisions; smaller cities would have fewer. No city would ever be divided in exactly this way for the best method of districting is to follow street lines. Whenever a division occurs at a particular street those on one side of the street would be in the district to which it belongs; those on the other side of the street would belong to the other district. Double lines indicate major district divisions; single lines indicate subdivisions.

| A | | B | | C | |
|---|---|---|---|---|---|
| 1 | 2 | 1 | 2 | 1 | 2 |
| 3 | 4 | 3 | 4 | 3 | 4 |
| D | | E | | F | |
| 1 | 2 | 1 | 2 | 1 | 2 |
| 3 | 4 | 3 | 4 | 3 | 4 |
| G | | H | | I | |
| 1 | 2 | 1 | 2 | 1 | 2 |
| 3 | 4 | 3 | 4 | 3 | 4 |

## ORGANIZATION PLAN

One general chairman

One secretary

Two vice-chairmen
  One for districts A through E
  One for districts F through I

A chairman for each district
  A chairman and three to six callers for each sub-district.

Callers report to their sub-district chairman on all calls made.
Sub-district chairmen report to the district chairmen.
District chairmen report to the vice-chairman for their group.
The two vice-chairmen report to the general chairman.

## SERVICES WHICH CALLERS MAY RENDER

Callers may be used for a variety of purposes. The first purpose, of course, is to keep in touch with the members of the church. If they have not been attending church regularly the callers can ascertain the reasons for non-attendance and encourage more regularity. Second, if there are situations of which the minister should be made aware, such as sickness, family trouble, poverty, or the like, they would report both to the minister and to their sub-district chairman. Third, they may be used to inform the members of special events, such as dinners, a preaching mission, or the like, encouraging people to come. Fourth, they can be used to reach new people who have moved into their neighborhood. They may secure the names of such people themselves or they may get them from the church office.

## A SPECIAL CALLING CARD

All visitors should be furnished with a special calling card giving the name of the church which they represent and introducing the visitor. Some cards are folded and list on the inside the hours of services, the church school hours, and other regular services of the church.

A sample card with the minimum essentials would be the following:

---

### THE WESTMINSTER PRESBYTERIAN CHURCH

Corner Fourth Street and Main


Introducing_____

We extend to you a cordial invitation to worship with us.

---

Callers should be instructed to present this card as soon as the party upon whom they are calling answers the door-bell. It is surprising how many church callers neglect even to mention the name of the church on whose behalf the call is being made; and it is, of course, possible for the householder to forget which church the kind people who called upon them actually represented.

## WHO SHOULD CALL?

Certainly it should be expected of every church officer that he will set aside some time each month to call upon either church members or prospects for membership. A church officer is in effect an under-shepherd. This is true of all denominations, whether they call their officers deacons, stewards, elders, or wardens.

They should also be concerned about the evangelistic program of the church for the command of Jesus Christ was to go into all the world and preach the Gospel to the whole creation. And He added, "beginning at Jerusalem." The application to the modern church, of course, would be "beginning where you are."

There are also in every church women who are particularly effective as callers. They may be members or officers of women's organizations or church school teachers.

In the Presbyterian Church of Scotland a very effective program is carried through preceding each communion service. Communion is held once each quarter and preceding it the elders call upon every member, the congregation being divided into districts. Elders make their calls in pairs and report back to the church on the results of their calls.

This program would be very effective if it were adopted in every church in America for it would insure four calls yearly upon the entire membership. There are other purposes for calls, however, which should also serve to integrate a congregation effectively.

## SUGGESTIONS TO CALLERS

So many jokes have been written about hospital calls that it seems unnecessary even to suggest techniques of visiting—whether in the home or hospital—but the fact remains that many callers do not understand some of the basic techniques of their work. Hence the following suggestions:

1. Routine church calls should always be short. By short we mean a maximum of half an hour. There are always exceptions to the rule. For instance a kind caller may find an opportunity in a busy household to help

with a task that the housewife is doing. But, aside from such exceptions, it is wise to limit the time spent on the call. A ten- or fifteen-minute visit may be even better than a half-hour.

2. There should always be a purpose in the call. Possibly it is to invite the person to come to church. Or it may be to extend an invitation to a particular function at the church—a woman's association meeting, a men's club dinner, or any other event. Under no circumstances should calling be aimless.

3. Avoid even the appearance of gossip. Avoid speaking about any disagreements which may exist within the church. If the person on whom the call is made is cognizant of some such circumstances and asks about them steer the converation away from such topics.

4. Avoid tactless statements or assertions concerning politics or religion. We have known callers, for instance, with strong Anti-Catholic prejudices who offended husbands or wives whose mates belonged to the Catholic church. The same would hold true of people of other denominations. It would be equally easy to make similar statements concerning political stands, or differences in nationality. The caller should have plenty to talk about concerning the purpose for which the call is made.

5. In hospital calls always be cheerful, but avoid an overly cheerful attitude. When visiting in a ward it is always in good form to introduce yourself to the other people there unless they are sleeping, reading, or visiting their own friends. Observe hospital rules as to time, availability of patients, etc. Generally speaking, there are particular rules for time of visits to wards and a more liberal policy for visiting private rooms. But, even though the nurse doesn't mention it, watch the patient to see that he is not tiring or is not overly exerting himself to respond to your conversation.

Never visit a hospital as part of a group. Two are the most who should ever make a hospital call together. And don't tell the patient about other people who are ill or about mutual friends who have recently died. There are surely more cheerful topics about which you can converse than those.

# 3

## INTEGRATING NEW MEMBERS
## AND GREETING STRANGERS

The story of altogether too many new church members is that they join a church, attend services regularly for a while, and then drop out. They have never been challenged to do something, never have been offered an opportunity to put their talents to work. They join the P.T.A. or a service club in their community and are given opportunities to go to work and, as a result, they become very much interested in these altogether worthy outside activities but gradually lose interest in the church.

A similar thing may happen to a person who is a newcomer in the neighborhood but has not joined a church. He goes to the church which he would normally join with his family but no one notices him. People greet other members and chat with them but he is left out. He feels strange. He feels that he is an outsider and after a few visits to the church he goes elsewhere. In the language of the day he "shops around."

To be sure, the church is not a social club. It is not created in order to afford recognition either to members or non-members for their abilities or talents. But, by the same token, it should offer people an opportunity to *do* something for the Kingdom. It should help people to channel their abilities into useful avenues of service. It should demonstrate needs for service and then offer people who are ready to serve the opportunity to go to work for Christ and the Kingdom.

And, although, as we have noted, it is not basically an organization for social intercourse, it should have the characteristics of a large family and an atmosphere of friendliness.

Some churches try to capture this family spirit in a totally artificial way. "Shake hands with three people you don't know," the minister remarks heartily every Sunday morning and beams at his congregation. Then everyone either ignores him — which makes the stranger or new member feel that the congregation is indeed unfriendly — or rushes around trying to find three unknowns who become overwhelmed by the greeting and never can remember the names of the people who introduced themselves.

## GREETINGS IN CHURCH

Far preferable to the very common procedure outlined in the last paragraph is to have a specially trained group who will be spotted throughout a church sanctuary and will be instructed to greet newcomers and secure their names and addresses. The "greet three people" has the aspect of forced hospitality. It is literally saying, "Our members are not friendly but we can coerce them to be." The latter method seems to be one of spontaneous hospitality. Someone has gone out of his way to greet a stranger or a new member.

27

Actually this arrangement is not spontaneous. It requires careful planning and occasional meetings with the responsible group. To make it effective the husband-and-wife teams which are appointed will be seated each Sunday in a designated area and will be responsible for from five to ten pews each. It will be their responsibility to meet the strangers and new members who are seated in their area, secure their names and addresses, and introduce them to others who may be seated in the same section. Immediately after the service they will turn over to the minister or the church secretary the cards and information on the strangers.

It is peculiar but true that people who begin to attend any particular church regularly will tend to gravitate to the pew or at least the general area in which they were seated the first time they came to church.

The great advantage of the plan for greeting which we have outlined is that by using it few of the new people will feel strange for very long. Each family begins to make some acquaintances in the new situation that they face. They feel that they are getting their roots down.

## PEW CARDS

Pew cards are generally effective only when they are used as attendance cards. That is, many strangers will hesitate to call attention to their strangeness by signing them. Some of the newcomers will, to be sure, but you don't get a complete roster of the strangers in this way. If, on the other hand, everyone, members as well as outsiders, is asked to sign a card to indicate his presence it is the most natural thing in the world for the stranger to join in doing something that *everybody* is doing.

It is very simple on Monday morning for the secretary to alphabetize the cards and then check through them for strangers. This method is also valuable for keeping in touch with the church-going habits of members. If a roster of attendance is kept, the minister will be able to note the families which probably need his pastoral services or calls by some of his church officers.

The strangers' cards can be turned over to the minister so that he can make calls upon them. By having squares to be checked the visitors-for-a-day can be segregated from new people who have moved into a church neighborhood so that the minister will not waste his time in calling upon the out-of-towner who is merely visiting for one Sunday.

The most effective calling program would be one in which a church member would make the initial call upon the visitor. If this plan is followed it would be wise to furnish visitors with report blanks so that they can indicate the results of their call. If they are fully familiar with the blank they can tactfully ask the questions which would provide the answers for the blank spaces without jotting down the answers until they have left the home. Among those which would normally be asked would be these:

28

1. Have these people established permanent residence in our neighborhood or are they just vacationing here?
2. What is their church affiliation?
3. Are they seeking a new church home or was their visit to our church merely a casual one? (If the card was signed on a rainy Sunday they might have chosen the church merely because it was in their neighborhood whereas their church would be one at some distance from their residence.)
4. Family information. Any children? Names and ages? Other relatives living with them?
5. Organizations in which they should be interested?

If a return call is indicated it could be made by the minister or one of his assistants if he has a staff. Certainly if these people are interested in joining the church they should be called upon immediately.

## WHEN NEWCOMERS JOIN THE CHURCH

Just as the first year is a critical one for every married couple the first six months or the first year is critical for the new church member. The church is presented with the alternatives of finding a niche into which the new member will fit or failing to integrate the person into the church.

In a large church it is especially essential that the new member be tied into some of the many activities in which the church is engaged, for it is manifestly impossible for the church to put that person to work in a position in the governing body of the church immediately after his or her reception. In the normal course of events it would probably be some years before the person would be considered for a church office.

But church organizations afford all interested people an opportunity to express themselves and find a place of service. It may be in the church school, the Boy or Girl Scouts, the women's organizations, the men's club, the church choir, the drama group, the young married group, or one of a host of different organizations. When they have found such opportunities for service the church becomes truly *their* church. The strangeness has worn off.

We advocate as the best plan for tying new members into the church program what we call the "buddy" plan.

## THE BUDDY PLAN IN OPERATION

In almost all of the swimming pools which are maintained by such organizations as the Boy Scouts, the Y.M.C.A. summer camps, etc., the "buddy" plan is carried out as a means of preventing drowning. Every boy is paired with another lad and each lad is expected to look out for the other.

Occasionally the director will blow a whistle and the buddies will pair up and lift their hands when they do so. This serves to remind them of their responsibilities for one another. No one can be lost in the milling crowd because each lad has a buddy who is always looking out for him. This plan cuts down casualties to a minimum in supervised swimming pools.

The buddy system will also cut casualties on church rolls to a minimum. Every family that joins the church has assigned to it another family which has been in the church for some time and whose members have all become a part of the church program. Father is a member of the Men's Club. Mother belongs to the Women's Society and is active in it. The children are in the Sunday School and youth groups.

The secret is to match up ages as well as possible so that young people of the same age as the youth members of the new family become responsible for the new young folks.

The older members are then instructed to invite the newcomers to attend various functions and meetings with them. They don't just extend them an invitation to go; they invite them to come along. It is even well to let the newcomers use their car on occasion and bring hot dishes or salads to pot-luck suppers. The purpose of the plan is not to carry the newcomers along on "flow'ry beds of ease" but to give them a working and serving part in the church and its various organizations.

As soon as the new members are thoroughly integrated into various parts of the church program they are assigned still newer members for whom they will be sponsors or buddies.

This has another interesting result. It widens the circle of friendship of all members, both new and old. At times it is advisable to join people of similar interests but there is also a value in crossing artificial social barriers, assigning a lawyer and his family to a garage mechanic and his children.

## WHEN SHOULD NEW MEMBERS PLEDGE?

There are two excellent ways of getting voluntary pledges from new members. It is highly important to have them tied into the church in their giving as well as in their presence.

The *wrong* way—but it is the easy way used by most churches—is to have the church treasurer mail the new member a box of offering envelopes. In so doing a very poor giving habit may be instilled from the very beginning. Very conscientious new members, conscious of their stewardship, may make regular and generous contributions but the vast majority of people who would receive such boxes would make merely nominal gifts since they had received no indication from anyone in the church as to its needs or its program. Nominal or token gifts of this kind range from 25 cents to $2.00. Only occasionally, as with old-age pensioners, is a contribution in this range a worthy one.

One way to secure pledges from all new members is to have a welcome dinner for them. Their opportunity to have a part in the work of the church through their giving would be only one item presented in the program, for representatives of the various organizations would also describe their activities and present their needs. Someone from the choir, a representative of the Men's Club, a representative from the Women's Association, from a youth group, from scouting activities, and so on would all be present to invite the new members to join them in their various programs.

Pledging would be one of these items. It might well be the last on the agenda and new members could be given an opportunity to make their pledges at the dinner if they desired or take their pledge cards home to be mailed in to the church later. The various activities of the church represented in giving should be frankly presented. "Our budget is this much,"—the amount should be given. "We are a strongly missionary church. We believe heart and soul in foreign and home missions. We support our Pension Board and our Board of Christian Education." If pledges are separately made for benevolences this should be pointed out so that the pledgers may have an opportunity to make pledges to these causes. It should be pointed out that their pledges should be made on the basis that so many Sundays remain in the year and the pledge covers only the balance of the year.

If the church has a current building fund pledge it should be pointed out that older members pledged for a period of two and one-half or three years for the new sanctuary or additional church school space but that they will be asked to make their pledges only for the months remaining in the payment period. They should definitely not be asked to sign pledges which would run beyond such a period.

The new members should not be embarrassed in any way and they should be advised that if they would like to take the pledge cards home with them so that they might make their decisions at leisure that would be perfectly all right. The suggestion should be made that pledges were promises to God and as such they might want to have a prayer before they signed them.

The other method is to have a committee from the church call upon the new members on some week night after they are received into the fellowship of the church. They could also take with them boxes of offering envelopes to hand the people as soon as they make their pledges. Whenever such calls are made they should present all of the financial appeals that will be made. People should not be called upon two or three times with different appeals.

## THE MARGINAL PEOPLE

Many churches which have large church school enrollments will have a large number of children in this department of the church's work whose parents do not belong to the church. They will bring their children to the church school on Sunday in the family automobile, drop them off, and pick them up again at the end of the hour. Many of these people have adopted the attitude that while the church is good for their children they no longer need it themselves.

They need to be convinced of their own need for the church and that they will have to set an example for their children if they hope that they will continue to go to the church school without their parents.

Sometimes economic circumstances enter in. The parents feel unable to contribute to the church because of stringent financial burdens and so feel embarrassed to come. Sometimes the mother is confined to her home with babies which make it difficult for her to attend.

These people do provide a field white to the harvest for earnest Christians. A calling schedule should be set up for every family in this category. The ice may well be broken by the church school teachers. If there are three children in the family there would be calls by three teachers. These should be followed up by others from the church who would be ready to press upon people their own needs for committing their ways to Christ and fellowshipping with other Christians.

A carefully organized calling program with these people as prospective members will always yield results. In another pamphlet we show how calls can be recorded and an accurate case history on every family can be kept. It is important to keep a record of some kind of these calls when they are made so that the minister or the chairman of the calling committee can see at a glance what has been done in each individual case.

## WIDENING THE PLEDGING BASE

We have always advocated calling upon everyone who has any contact with the church at the time of the every-member canvass. The results of such calls are remarkable. None of the non-members are ever told that it is their duty to give to the church nor is there a plea for a pledge. Instead they are informed of the privilege that is offered them to pledge to the support of the Christian enterprise. It is always a wise plan to offer them an opportunity to contribute to any church in which they might be interested; and the canvasser can say that he will be glad to send the pledge to the church of their choice if they would prefer to pledge to some other church than the one that he represents.

We have found that pledges are often the best means of evangelizing a family. It is easier for some business men to talk about pledges than it is to talk about the salvation of souls, but people often follow their pledges into the church fellowship.

The canvasser can also offer to call and take such people to church with him the following Sunday or invite them to other activities of the church and offer to bring them with him. Such an invitation as "Come to church next Sunday" is of little effect unless it is pinned down in some way. It is as meaningless as the invitation to come to dinner some time. A dinner invitation is only valid when it is to come on a specific night, at a specific time and an invitation to attend church is only real when a date is mentioned.

# 4

## A HANDBOOK FOR CHURCH USHERS

1. The Importance of Friendly Ushers
2. Uniformity of Attire
3. The Ushers' Stations
4. Greeters' Committee
5. Monthly Practice Sessions
6. The Act of Ushering
7. How to Take Up an Offering
8. Overflow Crowds
9. Diagrams

# A HAND-BOOK FOR CHURCH USHERS

## THE IMPORTANCE OF FRIENDLY USHERS

In a great many churches the single contact which the worshipers have with the church aside from attendance upon the church services is the usher or ushers who conduct them to their pews. If the usher's attitude is friendly, if he is helpful and courteous, the worshipers leave with a sense of warmth towards the church. If the usher is curt or oblivious to their presence they report later on that the church was cold and unfriendly.

Hence, the importance of choosing ushers carefully and training them in their duties. Many men would make excellent ushers if they understood what their duties were: and many good ushers render ineffective service because their group has not been properly organized.

The suggestions which are made in this booklet come out of actual experience over a great many years in the pastorate but they also come out of observation of many churches in which both ideal ushering arrangements and those which leave much to be desired prevail.

## UNIFORMITY OF ATTIRE

Ushers should be readily identifiable. For that reason it should be suggested to them that they be dressed in similar fashion if at all possible. The writer visited the old Roger Williams Church in Providence, R.I., on one occasion and found all ushers dressed in black cutaway coats with striped trousers and gray striped ties. The ushering in the church was perfect. The head usher greeted us at the door, turned us over to one of the ushers who served in one aisle. He preceded us to the pew, unlocked it, and then handed us a bulletin as he passed us in. This with a friendly smile.

The ushering in this historic Baptist church was actually better organized than the ushering in most New York City churches.

We are not going to suggest that all ushers buy cutaways and formal stiff collars but it is certainly not too much to expect the ushers in the average city churches to have blue serge or gabardine suits for ushering in the winter time. Further desirable standardization of attire would be to wear either gray and white striped ties, blue polk-a-dot ties, or some other similar neckwear, and black shoes. The minister is expected to dress in a certain manner and often pays a considerable amount of money for a heavy silk robe.

For summer wear we would suggest light gray or white suits with either black or white shoes. For every occasion, both summer and winter, if possible, it would be a good idea to have each usher wear a carnation or some other flower in his buttonhole. Again, whatever flower is chosen, all ushers should wear the same. This is preferable to name-plates and will always serve to designate an usher.

## THE USHERS' STATIONS

In every church one of the ushers should be designated as the head usher. He should be posted just outside the entry where he can greet people as they come in and direct them to the various aisles. He should keep in mind the seating and attempt to fill up each aisle uniformly if possible. Where there is more than one entrance the head usher should have a chief assistant stationed at each entry.

One usher should have a post at the head of each aisle and should be assisted by at least two ushers. It is his duty to hold visitors at the head of the aisle until one of his assistants can come back to take them to their pews. It would be well also if he could hold church members at this particular place but often members will want to find their own pews, especially if they are accustomed to sit in certain places. When members insist on finding their own seats it is sometimes difficult to persuade them to wait until another usher can find places for them.

When members do go past him he should give them their bulletins so that they will not have to pick them up after they are seated.

If ushers are trying to break up a long tradition of having members find their own places it is sometimes helpful to solicit the co-operation of the minister in requesting members as well as visitors to wait for the ushers. Naturally this must be done tactfully but it makes for an orderly situation in the aisles instead of a scramble for seats.

Under no circumstances should a stranger be permitted to come into the church without being welcomed by one or more ushers. Unfortunately, in some churches that does not occur. The usher enters into a conversation with some fellow-member and neglects the stranger. The wise usher will refrain from personal greetings to members which are time-consuming. The front door of the church is not the place for anecdotes.

## GREETERS' COMMITTEE

Some churches have organized greeters to welcome strangers and members. These people do not replace ushers nor is it their job to do the ushering. Their posts are at the door and they are there to greet people—not to show them to their pews. Often a greeters' committee will take the names of strangers on cards or invite them to sign a guest registry book.

There is, to be sure, a better way to get the names of visitors and that is to have a card in the pew which strangers can sign and place in the offering plate. When this method is used, it is highly important to call upon newcomers within the following week. In a large church the minister would ordinarily delegate this work either to an assistant or to a calling committee. If the callers should decide that a call by the minister would be desirable this can be arranged.

## MONTHLY PRACTICE SESSIONS

It is well to have occasional briefing sessions of the entire corps of ushers. This should be done when there are no people coming into the church. At such briefing sessions the procedure of ushering people to their seats and all of the other tasks for which the ushers are responsible should be followed. They should be letter-perfect in the important work of taking up the offering, bringing it forward for the offertory prayer, and also in aiding people to the door at the close of the service.

## THE ACT OF USHERING

In the practice sessions noted previously the head usher should permit one or more of the ushers to escort him to his pew in the sanctuary. It is always preferable to have the usher who actually places people give them their bulletins. It should be done just as he shows them to their pews.

Before starting down the aisle he should inquire of them whether they would like a place near the front, in the middle of the sanctuary, or farther back. If he wants to fill up the front pews his question should be phrased, "Would you like a seat near the front?" for that would usually elicit a "yes" response. If people prefer seats elsewhere they would so inform him, but they would generally agree.

The usher precedes the individual or the party that he is escorting and when he has reached the pew which he has chosen for them stands beside the pew just ahead. He motions for them to go in and hands them their bulletins as they pass him. He returns to the head of the aisle to get his next party. If they are coming down the aisle he would stop them courteously and ask if they would like to have him seat them.

Seating people is differently arranged when a sanctuary seems to be filling up on the one hand and when it is obvious that the attendance will nowhere nearly reach capacity proportions. When the sanctuary is going to be crowded the usher should courteously invite people to move towards the inside of the pew so that late-comers can be put into the outside places.

It is preferable under those circumstances to fill the pews nearest the pulpit first and the rear pews last. However, when the attendance is small a sanctuary can appear to be well-filled merely by spacing the people so that there will be several in each pew and very few or no empty pews. There is no reason at all to ask people to move in for they can be better reached with offering plates if they are at the ends and not in the middle of the pews.

Thereafter the usher should be responsible for this section of the sanctuary. In the event that someone is taken ill he should quickly make his way to the pew where the person is situated and render assistance. It is wise to know where the doctors are in the sanctuary so that they may be called upon if necessary. Assistance of this kind should be rendered quietly with as little interruption to the service as possible. Ordinarily the minister would continue the service. He can help to keep the congregation from getting excited by directing his glances to other areas of the sanctuary.

In the event of a fire or other such contingency the ushers would station themselves at previously determined posts in the aisles to assist in an orderly withdrawal. All exits should be used and the ushers should know the location of the exits.

The organ prelude is a part of the service but it is a period during which the vast majority of worshipers will be seated. The usher should go about his work quietly and efficiently and all conversation should be in muted tones or a whisper. If the usher is addressed by someone in a fairly loud tone of voice and will reply in a whisper the person who has thus spoken will lower his voice also.

After the invocation no one should be seated except at designated points in the service. These are often indicated by a series of stars thus: ****

Under no circumstances should the ushers ever leave the sanctuary during the course of a service for a smoke. Unfortunately, this is a common practice in some churches — particularly large ones. On a bright, sunny day immediately after taking the offering some ushers throng on the church steps for a brief smoke before returning to their duties. If an usher cannot get along without a cigarette for the period of the service he is certainly not the type of individual who should be given such an important assignment.

## HOW TO TAKE UP AN OFFERING

The usual procedure for an offertory is to have the ushers come forward to receive the offering plates from the minister. Sometimes the ushers receive the plates in the rear of the sanctuary and at the conclusion of the offering period present the plates to the minister. The former is definitely the preferable way and it makes of the offering more truly an act of worship.

We should not think of an offering, for instance, as a collection. An offering is a joint voluntary giving on the part of a congregation. A collection has implications of coercion and a business instead of a worship connotation.

The preferable way for ushers to come forward for the offertory is to have them march down the center aisle of the church in pairs if there is a center aisle. In those churches where there are two or four side aisles and no center aisle the ushers, again marching in pairs, should come down the aisles closest to the center. It is well to have the two inside men in the front rank set the pace, carefully watching each other so that they arrive at the rostrum simultaneouly. If, as is usual, they stand in front of the rostrum in either a single or double line, the men on the outside should then march down the outside aisles, the men on the inside down the inside aisle or aisles.

When there are stub aisles, as in the old-fashioned round auditorium type of sanctuary, the ushers who take these stub aisles ordinarily do not march down to the front. They take their stations and wait until the offering plates reach them from the outside aisles and then pass them across or start them back in the same section but in the pew back of the one from which they received the plates.

If a pew is largely empty with people sitting only at opposite ends the pew should be served by merely passing the offering plate to the individuals seated there, the usher retaining the plate in his own hands.

It is very awkward for someone to slide over in order to pass the plate to people at the other end of the pew.

As the ushers march back to their positions usually those farthest from the rostrum walk towards the back of the church. Each section of pews will be divided into areas of similar size. In a small church four men may be able to handle one section each. In a larger church it may require the services of six or eight men. In each case a group of ushers ordinarily take a prescribed section and move back until they have covered the section. When they have done so, they wait until the other sections are ready and then, at a signal from the head usher, march to the back of the church.

## OVERFLOW CROWDS

Many churches, with the resurgence of interest in church attendance, have resorted to duplicate or triplicate services. Churches which have taken this step almost universally report that the combined attendance of duplicate services always exceeds the attendance at single services.

Certainly if a church is regularly faced with an overflow crowd it would be advisable to take this step. It should ordinarily be the regular practice at Easter time.

This practice will go far to eliminate services where the "Standing Room Only" sign will have to be put out.

If, however, in the duplicate services there are overflow crowds, there are several steps which can be taken. It should be understood that no group of ushers should ever take upon themselves the decision as to how they will provide for additional seating. These decisions should always be reached after conferences with representatives of the municipal fire departments. These men know through study and experience what arrangements are safe and what are a menace to public safety.

If the fire department approves the following steps are possible:

1. A line of chairs just at the outside of a pew. If the fire department approves two, or three, or four such lines may be possible. They should be quietly put in place beginning in the front of the sanctuary as soon as the pews are filled. Proceeding from the front they should work towards the back of the sanctuary.

2. If, as in some churches, there is space back of the pews for additional lines of chairs they can be set in place there. Caution should be exercised never to block door ways.

3. As soon as the service is over the ushers should begin from the back to remove such chairs. It is easier to pass them from hand to hand than for one man to take one or two chairs, walk down the aisle where he would meet other men engaged in the same task, and prevent people from leaving by blocking the aisles.

## DIAGRAMS

On succeeding pages we present a few diagrams showing the arrangements for ushers in typical church sanctuaries, together with the manner of taking offerings in such churches. These can be enlarged for chart use when briefing sessions are carried out.

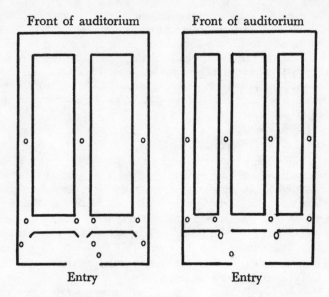

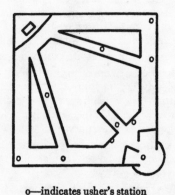

o—indicates usher's station

In the top two designs we have made no attempt to indicate pulpit or choir. They portray simply the aisles in the churches. In churches seating 900 or more there should be additional ushers for each aisle. The exact number needed can be worked out by experiment. It is important that there should be more ushers present at all times than are actually needed. The head usher can always hold one or more men in reserve.

# 5

## SUGGESTED APPLICATION FORMS
## FOR CHURCH MEMBERSHIP

# SUGGESTED APPLICATION FORMS FOR CHURCH MEMBERSHIP

In the light of a surge of religious interest in the second half of the twentieth century, churches, particularly those which are located in the suburbs and in new communities, are growing by leaps and bounds. There have been other such periods in the history of our country and often scores united with the church and were then lost in the shuffle.

Many churches are now facing the fact that new members may be lost unless they are carefully integrated into the church program. Pamphlet No. 3 in the set of Church Administration Pamphlets suggests means by which such integration can be accomplished. But a further step is necessary — careful classification of the applications for church membership. No longer do most churches consider it wise to accept immediately into membership the person who comes forward at the close of a service to profess his faith in Jesus Christ.

Such an individual may be a professional "joiner." Such a person may have no accurate conception of what it means to accept Christ as his personal Saviour and begin leading a Christian life.

The cards which we are suggesting are not intended to be used to *exclude* people from membership but to help them find their proper place in the life of the church and to enable the pastor to help them prepare to accept the responsibilities which church membership entails. In other words, these forms are designed to bring people into a *working* membership and not a rocking-chair church affiliation.

We will start with the simplest forms of membership applications and proceed to more elaborate types.

## THE SIMPLEST BASIS OF CHURCH MEMBERSHIP

As a basic form we would suggest the following:

### THE FIRST PRESBYTERIAN CHURCH OF KING CITY

#### APPLICATION FOR MEMBERSHIP

_____19____

To the Pastor and Session:

Sincerely confessing my faith in Jesus Christ as my Lord and Saviour and faithfully determining to pattern my life upon that of the Master I request that I may be received into active membership in The First Presbyterian Church of King City, Maine.

I desire to become a member on ☐ profession of faith; ☐ reaffirmation of faith; ☐ by transfer of letter from the_____Church of_____ _____the address of which is_____ _____

Applicants who are under nineteen years of age should check the following:

☐ I am_____years of age and understand that I must take a special training course and hereby agree to do so.

Signed:_____ Address_____

Phone Number_____

This form gives the basic facts concerning the prospective member and will serve for a small church, assuming that the minister will learn more about the applicant for his church file and will attempt to integrate the applicant into the life of the church. If this card is printed the material could go on a 4x6 card. If it is mimeographed, it probably would require a 6x8 card instead.

## SIMPLE FORM FOR A LARGER CHURCH

A second form which can also be put on a 4x6 card, using both sides is as follows:

## FRONT OF CARD

### THE SECOND CONGREGATIONAL CHURCH
#### WEBSTER, COLORADO
### MEMBERSHIP APPLICATION

_____ Phone_____
Please print name in full

Residence_____

☐ Single ☐ Married Woman's full maiden name_____

Husband's or wife's name _____

Preferred form of name for mailing list _____

Occupation or business _____

Business Address_____ Phone_____

Date of Birth: Month_____ Day_____ Year_____

Uniting by: Profession of faith_____Have you been baptized?_____

Reaffirmation_____

Letter from: _____
                Church              City              State

Plans for securing letter: ☐ Self ☐ Church office to write

## BACK OF CARD

What church work have you done?_____

What church offices have you held? _____

Names of children (with birth dates)

_____     _____
_____     _____
_____     _____

### OFFICE USE ONLY

Date_____ Information secured by:_____

☐ Women's Soc.          ☐ Church school          ☐ Couples
☐ Bus. & Prof. Wom.     ☐ Youth Groups           ☐ Men's Club
☐ Guild                 ☐ Young Adults            ☐ _____
☐ Service Groups        ☐ Young Matrons           ☐ _____

This is basically an information card but it is made out by anyone who plans to join the church. Usually, when a person joins by letter of dismission from another church the church office writes for the letter. Sometimes it is embarrassing, however, when the people who present themselves for membership come from a neighboring church. Under those circumstances it is proper to ask the prospective members to secure their own letters of dismission.

The information which is set forth at the bottom of the card is transmitted to the proper organizations with the request that they make calls upon the new members with a view to securing their integration in those organizations.

## A LONGER FORM

The type of church membership application which we would suggest, however, is much more complete than the other two. It contemplates a complete record of the person and it lists the basis for membership. It also presents the opportunities which the prospective members have for contributing to the support of the church.

While it is true that there is never an admission fee it is well to have the prospective member understand at the outset that one of the privileges as well as the duty of each member is to assume his share in the support of the church, the regular local budget and the missionary program as well. The longer form contemplates a pledge and enlistment in various church activities.

Following is such an application blank which should be published on two pages. It can be either mimeographed or printed as desired. It embodies everything that is needed to indicate a complete and wholehearted enlistment.

### APPLICATION FOR MEMBERSHIP
### FIRST METHODIST CHURCH, WINNETKA, ILL.

Date_____

It is my desire to become a member of the First Methodist Church by
_____Profession of Faith   Have you been baptized?_____
_____Reaffirmation of Faith

Former Church relationship_____
How long inactive_____ Any special reason_____
_____Transfer letter from_____

                        Name of church and complete
_____Shall we send for letter?_____
           Address
_____Reinstatement or Affiliation as Associate Member
Name of Home Church_____

### MY COVENANT WITH GOD AND THE CHURCH

In uniting with the First Methodist Church I make the following profession:

1. Believing in Jesus Christ as the Son of God, I accept Him as my own personal Saviour and acknowledge Him as Master and Lord.
2. Trusting in the Holy Spirit for guidance and help, I will endeavor to live a constant Christian life, honoring Christ in all my relationships, and seeking to know and obey the will of God in my home, my work, my recreation, and my citizenship.

As a member of this church

1. I will be faithful in my attendance upon its services.
2. I will render some form of Christian service.
3. I will give regularly by pledge for the support of the Church and its Benevolences as the Lord shall prosper me.
4. I will pray regularly for myself, for others, and for my church.

Signed

| First name | Middle name | Last name | (If married give husband's or wife's name) |

Address_____ Phone_____

Number and Street        City        Zone

Age group: Under 23___ 23-35___ 35-49___ 50-65___ Over 65___

Date of Birth_____ Date of Marriage_____

Month  Day  Year                    Month  Day  Year

Business Address (or School)_____Bus. Tel._____

Occupation_____ Firm Name_____

Relatives or persons (state relationship) who will know your changes of address.

1. In Winnetka _____

Name                                Complete Adress

2. Elsewhere _____

Name                                Complete Adress

INFORMATION ABOUT CHILDREN and/or OTHERS IN YOUR HOME (applicants under 23 are requested to give parents' names, address, and church membership in spaces below.)

| | NAME | ADDRESS | Birth Date | Baptizec' Yes or N | Church Membership |
|---|---|---|---|---|---|
| 1. | | | | | |
| 2. | | | | | |
| 3. | | | | | |
| 4. | | | | | |
| 5. | | | | | |

## OPPORTUNITIES AT FIRST CHURCH

I. What service did you perform in your former church?_____

_____

II. Have you held any church offices?_____

_____

III. My present activities in First Church_____

_____

IV. As a member of First Church I will be interested in:

CHRISTIAN EDUCATION DEPARTMENT

☐ Children's Department of Sunday Church School (ages 1-12)

☐ Wesley Fellowship Department of Sunday Church School (ages 12-23)
   ☐ Junior High  ☐ Senior High  ☐ College Age

☐ Young Adult Department of Sunday Church School (ages 23-35)
   ☐ Singles  ☐ Doubles (married)

☐ Adult Department of Sunday Church School
   ☐ Women's Class  ☐ Men's Class  ☐ Mixed Class

☐ Wesley Fellowship Clubs and Activities
   (Thursday afternoons, Sunday evenings)
   ☐ Junior High  ☐ Senior High  ☐ College Age

☐ Young Adult Clubs (Ages 23-35)
   ☐ Drama Club  ☐ Hikers' Club  ☐ Schooner Club (young married)  ☐ Games Program  ☐ Reading Club

- [ ] Scouting
  - [ ] Cubs  [ ] Brownies  [ ] Boy Scouts  [ ] Girl Scouts
  - [ ] Senior Scouting (Boys)  [ ] Senior Scouting (Girls)
- [ ] Mothers' Council (for mothers of children 1-11)

## WOMEN'S DEPARTMENT
- [ ] Missionary Society  [ ] Afternoon Guilds  [ ] Evening Guilds
- [ ] Aid Society
- [ ] First Methodist Business Girls' Club
- [ ] Leadership in Girls' Classes, Clubs, Activities
- [ ] Red Cross Unit Work

## MEN'S DEPARTMENT
- [ ] First Methodist Men's Club
- [ ] Ushering  [ ] Morning Service  [ ] Evening Service  [ ] Special
- [ ] Bowling League
- [ ] Leadership in Boys' Classes, Clubs, Activities
- [ ] Every Member Canvass

## MUSIC DEPARTMENT
- [ ] Children's Choirs  [ ] Choir Mothers  [ ] Wesley Fellowship Choir  [ ] Choir Mothers  [ ] Cathedral (Adult) Choir  [ ] Sunday Evening Choir  [ ] Summer Choir  [ ] Pianist  [ ] Organist
- [ ] Other Instrument  [ ] Vocal Soloist for organizational meetings  [ ] Song Leader

## SPECIAL SERVICES
- [ ] Dramatics. Any particular phase? _____
- [ ] Leadership in Boys' Classes, Clubs, Activities
- [ ] Leadership in Girls' Classes, Clubs, Activities
- [ ] Visiting for the Church: Sick and Shut-in
- [ ] Providing Transportation: Shut-in services for callers
- [ ] Hobby and recreational skills: Describe_____
  _____

- [ ] Volunteer Care in Nursery and Crib Rooms:
  - [ ] Sunday  [ ] Special Occasions
- [ ] Telephoning for the Church:  [ ] At Church  [ ] At home
- [ ] Volunteer Office Work:
  - [ ] Typing  [ ] Stenography  [ ] Mimeographing
  - [ ] Filing  [ ] Preparing Mailings  [ ] Other
- [ ] Libraries
- [ ] Opening home for church groups
- [ ] Offering Professional Services
  (for needy or for service to Church)
  - [ ] Medical  [ ] Dental  [ ] Legal  [ ] Other
- [ ] Volunteer Help for special projects
  - [ ] Publicity  [ ] Posters  [ ] Photography  [ ] Planning
  - [ ] Painting  [ ] Carpentry  [ ] Electrical  [ ] Toy Repair

☐ Other Service Tasks: _____

If this long form is used additional special forms should be set up for every category in IV above. This could take the following form:

## DRAMATICS

| Name | Address | Dates | | |
|------|---------|-------|---|---|
| | | Information Received | Given to Club | Joined |

If the dramatic program is not organized but people are used for special dramatic presentations then this list would be set aside until a play or pageant was given and all who had signed up would be notified of the forthcoming event.

The same would hold true of integration into the Church School, the Men's or Women's Departments, Music, etc. If the information is secured it should be used.

# 6

## THE INGREDIENTS OF AN EFFECTIVE WORSHIP SERVICE

# THE INGREDIENTS OF AN EFFECTIVE
# WORSHIP SERVICE

Some years ago when Dr. Charles M. Sheldon, author of the most widely read best-seller of all time, "In His Steps," was a guest in the home of the author, he asked him how he planned his morning services and after listening for a time to the author's outline he made the interesting suggestion, "Why don't you start your service occasionally with the sermon and have your worship period last? You probably have some members who plan to arrive just in time for the sermon and if you change your service so that the sermon comes first on some occasions they will get into the habit of coming on time for fear that they will miss your message."

He added, "You know, of course, that there is nothing especially sacred about the form of service that you use. It's just a matter of custom." Dr. Sheldon was seventy-nine years old at the time that he made that observation but he was constantly changing the form of service in his own First Congregational Church of Topeka, Kansas, and bringing freshness not only to his preaching but also to the worship experience.

## A FEW OBSERVATIONS

It should be noted at once that Dr. Sheldon had put his finger upon a definite weakness in many Protestant services. If worshippers were bored by what they regarded as "the preliminaries" then certainly they were not vital. If a service always followed a certain pattern, the repetition of certain phrases or prayers, the singing of certain hymns, the singing of an anthem which seemed merely like an opportunity for the soprano and tenor to show the quality or lack of quality of their voices, it was not to be wondered that people stayed away from the services, at least for the portion of the hour devoted to such practices.

If the prayers of the minister were so stereotyped that the worshippers always knew what he was going to pray for next and if such prayers had no relationship to their own needs and aspirations then, indeed, was change needed.

## THE ELEMENTS OF THE WORSHIP SERVICE

There are certain elements which should be included in a worship service. That does not mean that all of those elements should be present in every worship service but they should be included at least occasionally.

These elements are:
   A. Ascription of deity to God.
   B. Confession of sin.
   C. Assurance of pardon.
   D. The teaching of the Word — through preaching.
   E. The element of sacrifice — through the presentation of the offering.
   F. Prayer. (This is essentially communication with God and is only effective as through this means the worshippers feel the presence of The Eternal in their midst.)

## AVOID THE STEREOTYPED

When a service is so arranged that the same things are said every Sunday at exactly the same time and in the same way the service is in danger of becoming a "vain repetition" against which Jesus particularly warned His disciples.

The so-called "Lord's" prayer (it should be designated as the "apostles' " prayer since it was one which Jesus taught His disciples to use in their own devotions) is especially in danger of misuse through undue familiarity. If it always comes after the invocation and if it is merely repeated, always in the same cadence, always in the same way, it often becomes meaningless. People can "say" the Lord's prayer without "praying" it.

There are several ways in which real content can be put into the prayer. One is to vary the time when it is used. Another is to introduce it with a short word of explanation. Another is to suggest that the prayer be prayed with brief pauses between the different phrases so that they may be allowed to sink in. Sometimes it would be well to pray it with the minister filling in the pauses with a brief elaboration of its meaning. We set out below one of the ways in which the prayer may be prayed, using only the opening phrases:

"Our Father who art in heaven — Pause — 'We have only one God, a loving Father, whom we acknowledge as supreme' — Pause —

Hallowed be Thy name — Pause — 'We cannot make the name of God hallowed or sacred. His own holiness sanctifies His blessed name' — Pause —

Thy kingdom come — Pause — 'In Thy own good time we know that Thy kingdom will be established in our midst' — Pause —

Thy will be done on earth as it is in heaven — Pause — 'But make us to know, O Father, that *we* must do Thy will if Thy will is to be supreme here on earth' . . ."

We are inclined to believe that the Lord's prayer should be used in every service but it must be made vital and never under any circumstances should we make the customary suggestion, "We will now *say* the Lord's prayer."

There is very little justification for using the Apostles' creed in every service. If a statement of faith is to be used it would be well to vary it, using various statements of our basic faith to be read by the congregation, or perhaps elaborating upon a single article in the creed.

There are great creeds in poetry as well and these can be read in lieu of the Apostles' creed. Among them are the following:

"Providence" — William Cowper

"To God" — Robert Herrick

"Waiting" — John Burroughs

"There Is No Unbelief" — Elizabeth York Case

"With Whom Is No Variableness, Neither Shadow of Turning" — Arthur Hugh Clough

"The Tide Of Faith" — George Eliot

"The Stream Of Faith" — William Channing Gannett

"A Song Of Faith" — Josiah Gilbert Holland

These are only a few of the many poems which can be used in this way and thus enrich the lives of worshippers. Since these poems express a tremendous faith they open up various aspects of the creed. The Apostles' creed should be used on occasion but it should always be introduced by a stirring announcement such as, "Now let us make confession of our faith," or "Let us proclaim our belief in the great truths of our holy religion."

## THE OFFERING

Strange to say there are still ministers who announce that "We will now take up the collection." Even such a statement as "We will now receive the offering" is not wholly adequate although it is preferable to the former.

Since the offering is an act of worship, since it takes the place of the sacrifices which Jews offered in the temple service, this fact should be noted with some such phrase as, "Let us now worship God in laying our offerings upon the altar," or "Giving is a act of worship. We bring our sacrifices as did worshippers of old and place them upon the altar. The envelopes which are put on the offering plates represent our toil and our sacrifice. Let us, therefore, give as an act of worship."

When the writer was overseas as a chaplain, although he served the air force, he was a civilian with primary responsibility for civilians who were working at a huge air base in North Ireland. Offerings were received at all services but all of the money received was used for others and not for the support of the chapel. Both soldiers and officers came to him in considerable numbers to say that one of the most significant things about the chaplain's services were the opportunities afforded to make offerings: they had missed participating in the service through the offerings at the regular military establishments where they had served. Since this is such a vital part of the service, therefore, it deserves to be made an act of worship and dedication.

## PROTESTANT CONFESSIONALS

More and more churches are adopting public prayers of confession which have long been used in Episcopalian churches. They are printed in church bulletins and at the proper place in the service they are read aloud together. They are followed by the minister's words of assurance of pardon.

Lacking space in a bulletin and having no such expression of contrition in the hymnal or in some other printed form the minister may yet give an opportunity to the worshippers to express their penitence for sin and their desire for pardon by inaugurating a quiet time when each one in his own way, quietly before God, will seek God's forgiveness for sin. The minister may use a directed prayer with frequent moments of silence and then end with the assurance of pardon.

## THE SERMON

A word regarding the sermon is not out of place at this point. Unequivocally we would state that a sermon is not a book review: it should not be a diatribe against members of another or other faiths: it ought not to be a discussion — no matter how intelligent — of national or international problems. A challenging book may sometimes form the *basis* for a sermon and occasionally the pulpit must speak out on the issues of the time when they have moral and spiritual implications, as, for instance, on the issue of racial tolerance, the indiscriminate use of the hydrogen bomb, evils in the body politic, and other similar issues. But whenever the pulpit speaks out in this manner it should never be along partisan lines. It should be solely on moral and spiritual implications of momentous problems.

Basically the sermon should meet people where they are. It should suggest the Christian solution to the problems which men, women, and children meet every day in their lives. Esoteric themes, totally unrelated to the temptations and difficulties which people face day by day, although they may give a minister a reputation for scholarly achievement cannot help the people in the pew to live their lives in home, on the schoolground, in the shop and office.

## ARRANGING THE FORM OF THE SERVICE

We have suggested the basic ingredients for the worship service in our paragraphs on "The Elements Of The Worship Service." Now as to their arrangement. There is no reason why the sermon should not come first in a service, immediately after the introit and the invocation, possibly with a hymn, which is related to the theme which the minister will develop.

There is no good reason either for always putting the offering just before the sermon. Often it should come last, the final act of worship in a warm, Spirit-filled service.

Someone remarked — it has been ascribed to Henry Ward Beecher but most of his sermons that I have read required forty minutes to an hour just for reading — that "no one was saved after the first twenty minutes of preaching."

There is little point in trying to arrange for a sermon which is exactly twenty minutes in length. Some themes require more and some less time than that. But there is considerable virtue in building a service which is well timed. Most churches find that the acceptable length for a service will vary from one hour to an hour and fifteen minutes. This includes the organ prelude which is often fifteen minutes long.

When the prelude is of that length it goes without saying that the church organist should be a person who can put feeling into the playing of his or her instrument. The prelude should set the mood for the service, sometimes quiet, sometimes challenging and heroic.

And now concerning announcements, the depth of banality. There may be need occasionally for an announcement of some special nature. It may be a meeting of such tremendous importance that the minister will want to call attention to it in a very brief word. But there is little virtue in announcing twice monthly that the sewing circle will meet on Wednesday afternoon and a very pleasant two hours followed by tea and crumpets will be enjoyed by those who attend. And certainly the minister should not call attention weekly to the fact that the church is growing rapidly but more members are needed. Hence he will be happy to meet you after the service and talk with you regarding church membership.

The only place where announcements are excusable is in the little country or city church which cannot afford to print or mimeograph a bulletin weekly. And it is quite probable that they are not needed in such a church since the members of the organizations are all aware of the time of their meetings.

# THE BASIS OF THE ARRANGEMENT OF A SERVICE

The basic principle for arranging a service is that every phase of it shall have spiritual meaning and content, that all phases will point to some type of commitment, that they will press for certain vital decisions. Such decisions may assume a number of different forms. One Sunday the minister may strive to bring the people to the point where they will banish anxiety. On another occasion he may seek to inculcate new standards of honesty in dealing with neighbors, competitors, customers, employers, or employees. On still another he may press for a decision to give their hearts to God.

On occasion the pastoral prayer should come after the service. If a stirring anthem is desired which will give a mood of commitment to the congregation it may follow the sermon. It goes without saying that no solo or anthem should be sung merely to give the choir or a soloist the opportunity to exercise his talents.

The traditional churches could learn much from the Salvation Army and the revivalists where every song is one which has as its purpose commitment of life. They are usually Gospel songs which traditionalists regard as trite but they do have a message which is understood by the hearers. Yet the church hymnal is full of hymns which have just as vital messages and there are anthems which stir the very soul of the hearers.

## A HYMN OF THE MONTH

As a final suggestion we would advise a careful perusal of the Hymnal to ascertain what hymns are rarely sung by the congregation, largely because they are unfamiliar and yet have rich content. The hymnody of some congregations is often confined to approximately twenty to twenty-five songs. Yet the Hymnals of most churches are filled with great songs which congregations should learn.

When such hymns are discovered it is well to have them introduced to the congregation with a "Hymn of the Month" program. When a song is announced as the "Hymn Of The Month" it is first played in its entirety by the organist and then sung by the choir. The next Sunday the entire congregation is invited to sing it and so on for the succeeding weeks of the month. By the end of the month it will have become familiar to all and a part of their melodic vocabulary.

# 7

## THE IMPORTANCE OF APPROPRIATE PULPIT ATTIRE

1. Gowns Now Almost Universal
2. Clerical and Academic Gowns
3. When Wearing Gowns
4. The Use of Stoles
5. When Should a Gown Be Used
6. Choir Robes
7. Styles of Gowns

# THE IMPORTANCE OF
# APPROPRIATE PULPIT ATTIRE
## (Gowns, Hoods, Vestments)

There have been two schools of thought in recent times regarding the use of gowns in the pulpits of American churches, and also, earlier in the century, regarding the wearing of Prince Albert and cutaway coats. The nonconformist tradition was that anything savoring of special attire for the clergy was out of place. A minister was like any other lecturer or speaker. He should be attired as any other business man would be. In a sense it was also a frontier tradition. A church was any place where a crowd of people could be assembled. It might be a schoolhouse or a grove or even a barroom (with the bar temporarily suspending operations.)

The other tradition was the episcopal one. A minister was a priest and in his priestly function his garb should be different. It should somehow identify him with his office.

In the British Isles the episcopal idea won out long ago and the clergy of even the lowest of the nonconformist groups were won over to the idea that when a man was at the sacred desk he should be attired in such a way that he would be recognized as a minister of the Gospel. Consequently the ministers of the British Isles almost universally wear a rabat and clerical collar, whether they are Anglicans, Methodists, or Presbyterians. Some of the Baptist and Congregational clergymen prefer to dress in business garb but most of them are attired in a black suit, black tie, and starched collar when they go into the pulpit, differing from some of their brethren in this country who go in for decided informality of dress and may even wear ties of the brightest hues.

## GOWNS NOW ALMOST UNIVERSAL

Gowns are now almost universal in the pulpits of America with the exception of the Pentecostal sects where they are still frowned upon, but the trend towards pulpit vestments is fairly new and, in consequence, there is a wide diversity of usage. There are, for instance, men who hold only bachelor's degrees who will purchase doctor's gowns for pulpit use: and there are still some men who will wear brown or sports oxfords with their gowns.

Certainly uniformity is not essential; but good taste is. We have heard of a very prominent clergyman who, when preaching a trial sermon for one of the great pulpits of America, lost a call because of the fact that he wore brown trousers and tan shoes with black vestments. It was conceded by all that he would have received the call if he had been differently attired.

He took the setback gracefully but at subsequent ministers' meetings he warned his brethren against such informality and advised them to observe traditions of attire. He rightly insisted on a minister's call to preach as he believed but suggested that when one was in Rome it was best to don Roman garb.

## CLERICAL AND ACADEMIC GOWNS

Clerical and academic gowns are worn almost interchangeably today. There is no particular reason, therefore, why a minister should not wear his academic gown in the pulpit if he so desires but a man who holds a bachelor's or master's degree should not, of course, wear a doctor's gown or a doctor's hood. On the other hand, a man who holds a doctor's degree could wear an ordinary pulpit gown without the doctor's facings without giving offense in any way since he is not sailing under false colors.

Most Episcopal clergymen wear cassock, surplice, and stole. Lutherans wear a closed front style gown with standing collar and wide front pleats which create the effect of a cassock front.

The choice for other ministers would normally be between an open front gown (usually called a Geneva gown) and a closed front gown. If a man holds a doctor's degree, either earned or honorary, he is entitled to wear velvet chevrons on his sleeve. Generally they are black but they may be the color of the department in which the degree was granted. Scarlet, for instance, would be the color for the degree of doctor of divinity or doctor of theology. A man holding the degree of doctor of laws would have purple chevrons, a doctor of philosophy blue chevrons, etc.

However, as we have indicated, the usual practice is to have black velvet chevrons and black velvet panels down the front. The black velvet panels without chevrons may be worn by a minister who does not hold the doctor's degree.

More and more ministers are wearing academic hoods with their gowns. Here again they will want to secure the hood to which they are entitled. If they have a bachelor's degree they would wear a bachelor's hood which is the smallest of the three. A master's hood is slightly larger, and a doctor's hood the largest of all. Most ministers have degrees from several institutions and they may therefore, wear any hood to which they are entitled or they may alternate between their various hoods.

Gowns are not necessarily expensive. In fact, the less expensive gowns are actually more comfortable since they are usually of a lighter weight than the heavier and more expensive gowns. The price range usually begins at about twenty-five dollars for the most simple gowns and the top price is generally a little over one hundred dollars.

If gowns are desired for summer wear we would suggest the use of one in a light color. While gowns are made in a variety of colors the light gray, suntan, and maize are particularly effective. We do not advise a white gown for it soils so very quickly that it is almost necessary to dry-clean it weekly.

## WHEN WEARING GOWNS

Whenever gowns are worn which have an open front a minister should either wear a detachable front panel, a vest, or a rabat. There should not be an expanse of white shirt showing. Whenever a gown is worn which is closed in front it is not necessary, of course, to wear a vest.

When a minister has a suit which does not possess a vest it will be necessary, of course, to wear the suit coat. If one of the light color gowns is worn in summer it should be in conjunction with a suit of similar color. In the winter it would be permissible to wear a dark blue suit as well as a black suit with black or black-and-white striped trousers. It would be a mistake to wear a brown or variegated gray suit.

Naturally with a black gown the minister would never wear any shoes other than black. For a white gown a white suit would be preferable and white shoes. Brown or tan shoes can be worn with a suntan or maize gown for summer wear. On any other occasion it would be a mistake to wear them.

Some ministers are led astray in their wearing of gowns by the informal way in which they are occasionally worn on college campuses. Some very individualistic professors will wear tweeds and brown shoes to commencement, but you will notice that the university president and the commencement speaker is never so attired.

The point to bear in mind is that a commencement is a formal service and college professors should also remember that—no matter how desirous they are of emphasizing their independence. The most individualistic professor, for instance, would never under any circumstances wear a pair of tan shoes with a tuxedo or full dress, yet the function which he would be attending requiring such garb would be far less formal than a university commencement.

The basic idea of the gown, of course, is to serve as a badge of one's office and whether a gown is worn or not the fundamental principle is that a minister in his pulpit should be attired in clothing of subdued colors. A sunburst necktie may be all right for wear in business or to the race track but it is definitely out of place in the church sanctuary.

## THE USE OF STOLES

Most of the chaplains in the United States Army, whatever their rank or denomination, became accustomed to the use of stoles with various Christian symbols. These were primarily worn with the uniform in the field where they became the symbol of the minister's preaching and especially his priestly function in the distribution of the elements at communion.

When the chaplains returned to duty in the States they had become so accustomed to their use that they adopted them for use with their gowns as well. After they had been discharged from the Army they continued to use them so that the stole has come into fairly universal acceptance. There are a variety of symbols which can be used effectively but in all probability the most beautiful are the simplest ones with either the Latin or the Greek cross superimposed upon them.

## WHEN SHOULD A GOWN BE USED?

This pamphlet has not been designed to suggest that all ministers should wear gowns or stoles although their use has now become fairly common in most Protestant churches. On two occasions the writer introduced the use of the gown in congregations where he served. There was some opposition at first but later on even the opponents of the idea were won over and acknowledged that the use of the gown gave a dignity to a service which was lacking, at least in part, without it.

Gowns should not be worn for informal services, as, for instance, a prayer-meeting service where the atmosphere should be basically one of complete informality. But a gown may be worn for a home or garden wedding and be perfectly suited to the occasion. It may be worn at funerals, both in the mortuary chapel, the home, or the church, and also at the grave.

## CHOIR ROBES

The minister might tactfully suggest to the choir leader that uniformity might be desirable in the choir loft as well as in the pulpit. Very often the appearance of a solemn processional is marred by reason of the fact that there is so much variation in the dress of the people in the choir below the hems of the gowns which they wear.

Suggested for choir use would be low-heeled black shoes with black or blue gowns, white shoes for white gowns and black shoes for gowns with white cassocks. Junior choir members ought to wear stockings instead of bobby sox. Unfortunately, little can be done with over-elaborate hair-dos but uniformity should be achieved in the wearing of hose and footwear.

If the suggestions are tactfully made and the reasons for them are explained to members of the choir there will be little difficulty in securing the co-operation of the singers.

## STYLES OF GOWNS

The various simple styles of gowns for ministers are illustrated below together with stoles. You can consult your church vestment house for hoods. When writing about hoods list the degree that you hold and the college which granted it and the firm will send you full information as to prices, etc.

The Episcopal gown          A doctor's gown (academic)

A Lutheran gown                    The Geneva gown

# 8

## A NEW LISTING SYSTEM FOR MEMBERS, PROSPECTS, AND SUNDAY SCHOOL PARENTS

1. Attendance Card and Attendance Record
2. The Monday Morning Check-off
3. Church Prospects
4. Keep Up the Files
5. Addressograph Plates
6. Prospects
7. Attendance Record

# A NEW LISTING SYSTEM FOR MEMBERS, PROSPECTS, AND SUNDAY SCHOOL PARENTS

We are presenting here a system which has proved remarkably successful in every church where it has been put to work. It is so simple that it will take comparatively little time to make the proper entries weekly and it will pay off in keeping track of the church participation of all of the members as well as finding the prospective members and following up on them.

All of the forms presented here can be mimeographed in the church office or printed if the church prefers. Aside from the 3 x 5 and 4 x 6 cards plus some packages of mimeograph paper the only supplies needed to inaugurate this system will be some card file cabinets and one or more 8½ x 11 3-hole loose-leaf notebook covers. The cost to the average church for installing the system will probably be less than ten dollars.

## ATTENDANCE CARD AND ATTENDANCE RECORD

We have discovered that one of the finest means of securing the names of potential members is by the use of attendance cards. Where we have had to introduce this to a congregation not already using it we have invariably encountered some opposition on the part of church officers and older members. They usually grumble at the idea that they should be asked to sign a card every Sunday indicating that they have been in church.

The fact remains that usually visitors and non-members will fail to sign cards of this nature which are in use in most churches unless *everybody* signs a card. If visitors or non-members only are asked to sign cards they very often fail to do so since by so doing they proclaim the fact that they are strangers. Hence the value of having everyone in attendance sign a card.

By so doing the minister is also able to discover who in his congregation failed to attend church. He can follow up such non-attendance at his own discretion. If some older person who regularly attends should miss a service he may want to have a calling committee check by telephone, have his secretary do it, or do so himself.

## THE MONDAY MORNING CHECK-OFF

The two forms for recording attendance are the card which is reproduced herewith (Form #1), and the page (Form #2), which is found at the back of this pamphlet. A short announcement just before the offering is received asking everyone to sign an attendance card, will be sufficient on Sunday. The cards can then be received with the offering.

On Monday morning the cards are alphabetized and the entries made on Form #2. There is room for six names on a page and these should be entered alphabetically.

## ATTENDANCE CARD

Name_____Phone No._____

Address_____

### PLEASE CHECK BELOW

| Member | Visitor From Out of Town | Desire to Unite with Church | Newly Ar- rived in Community | Desire Pas- toral Call |
|--------|--------|--------|--------|--------|
|        |        |        |        |        |

Comment:_____

_____

Provision can be made for new members by skipping every third blank so that new members can be listed in the vacant spaces or by adding pages as needed. The alphabetical order cannot be completely accurate but by inserting pages as required it will not be very wrong. For instance, if Mr. and Mrs. Halsted join the church after the book is made up a new page can be inserted in a loose leaf book under the "H" designation which will put them in their approximate order. It would be well to enter name, address, and telephone number for each member so that in checking the roll a 'phone call can be made from this roll instead of referring to some other.

Form #3 is a suggested membership card which lists the basic facts regarding the member's family. It is suggested that it be made in duplicate so that the pastor can have one set of cards for use in his calling and the other set should never be taken from the office for any purpose. The cards will be identical in every respect.

These forms should be mimeographed on white 4 x 6 cards and filed alphabetically. It is always wise to use alphabetic dividers for files for convenience in locating the cards.

In the average family the father's name will be listed on Line No. 1 above, the Mother's name on Line 2, and the children in order of their age on Lines 3, 4, 5, 6, 7 and 8. These numbers will then be placed in the boxes below which indicate participation in church activities. Thus if the father is a church officer, a member of the men's club, and a member of the troop committee of the Boy Scouts his number would appear in each of those boxes. If a son is in church school, a member of a youth group, and a scout his number would appear in the appropriate box. Space should be left in front of each name for an "M" if the individual is a member of the church.

**MEMBERSHIP CARD**    M indicates member  _____
                                             Phone No.

Last Name                        Address

_____(1)          _____(5)

_____(2)          _____(6)

_____(3)          _____(7)

_____(4)          _____(8)

**PARTICIPATION**

| Men's Club | Women's Ass'n | Church School | Youth Groups | Boy Scouts | Girl Scouts | Church Office | |
|---|---|---|---|---|---|---|---|
|  |  |  |  |  |  |  |  |

Joined Church_____By_____

Employment_____

Comment_____

Record of calls on other side

Since these cards are made up in duplicate, one for the church file and one for the pastor, he can refresh his memory by a quick glance at the card before he makes a call. On the back of the card, in addition to the notation concerning the time of the visit, the minister may want to make some pertinent comment which he would have only on his own card. He should place a bracket with "Pr." after such comment to indicate that it is a private notation. If it is a comment which can appear on the card in the church file he would leave it without such a notation.

After the previous day's calls the minister or his secretary should make appropriate entries in the office file cards.

Since the above card lists all members of a family, whether or not they are members of the church it is advisable to have another file on 3 x 5 cards for church members only. This would be an individual file card, one for each member. It can be as simple as the following:

**FORM #4**

Name_____

Address_____

_____

Received into church membership_____

Separated from church membership _____

By_____

The notation "Separated from church membership" would be followed by the date and after "By" a notation concerning the way in which membership terminated. If it was by death, by dismissal to another church, by suspension, or by some other method the proper notation should be made. In the event that it was by letter of dismission the name of the church to which the letter was issued should be included.

Two 3 x 5 file boxes are needed for these cards. One will be used for the active members and the other will be used to store the cards of those whose membership has terminated.

In the event that there is a desire to segregate the "suspended" members it would be well to have a third file box for this purpose. When such a file is maintained it is generally done so that suspended members may be called upon occasionally in the hope that they may resume active membership.

Most churches have purchased from their denominational headquarters membership books. Entries in the membership roll are made chronologically and a number is ordinarily assigned. If such a number is given the same number should appear in the upper right-hand corner of Form #4. If no such numbers are given then the Page Number should appear in that place.

## CHURCH PROSPECTS

A handy form of dividing church prospects into two categories is made on the basis of family participation in church school activities. If children are in the church school we use a pink card to designate the family and a green or blue card to designate prospective members who are not identified with the church school.

These two cards are similar in every respect to the membership cards with the exception of the designation "PROSPECT CARD" instead of "MEMBERSHIP CARD". The prospect cards for the two categories which we have proposed are printed in exactly the same way but the colors suggested above are used to differentiate between them. The use of color also makes it possible for the minister to tell by merely glancing at the color of the card whether the people on whom he is calling are members or non-members.

These cards, as with the membership cards, should be made out in duplicate. It would be well, however, to have an attendance record mimeographed on the back of the card so that the minister may know when these people began to attend church and how regular their attendance has been. We would suggest that the attendance record should be made up in the same way as for Form #2.

## KEEP UP THE FILES

It may appear like something of a chore to keep up the records which we have suggested. Actually it will require only a few minutes time daily and the rewards of such bookkeeping are tremendous. From the attendance record the minister can tell at a glance which members are in need of special help or cultivation and the file of green and pink cards will keep ever in his mind the membership potential with which he has to work.

## ADDRESSOGRAPH PLATES

When invitations are sent to church affairs they should always be sent to Mr. and Mrs. George Smith although only one of the two is a member of the church unless there are special reasons why the non-member should not be included.

## PROSPECTS

Referring once more to Form No. 1, all prospect cards which are received should be carefully scrutinized to ascertain if possible whether the people who came to church on a particular Sunday were just visitors from a distance or were people seeking a church home.

If the latter, the minister or the calling committee should see them at once. A simple assignment card for calls would be the following:

## FORM #5

M_____ _

_____

Address

Phone_____

Were recent visitors at our services. We would appreciate it if you would call on the prospect and report the results of your call on the back of this card.

These people may be potential candidates for membership in

_____

The last sentence of this form refers to some specific church organization in which the person making the call may himself or herself be interested.

## FORM #2
## ATTENDANCE RECORD

| Jan. | Feb. | Mar. | Apr. | May | June | July | Aug. | Sept. | Oct. | Nov. | Dec. |
|------|------|------|------|-----|------|------|------|-------|------|------|------|
|      |      |      |      |     |      |      |      |       |      |      |      |
|      |      |      |      |     |      |      |      |       |      |      |      |
|      |      |      |      |     |      |      |      |       |      |      |      |
|      |      |      |      |     |      |      |      |       |      |      |      |

| Jan. | Feb. | Mar. | Apr. | May | June | July | Aug. | Sept. | Oct. | Nov. | Dec. |
|------|------|------|------|-----|------|------|------|-------|------|------|------|
|      |      |      |      |     |      |      |      |       |      |      |      |
|      |      |      |      |     |      |      |      |       |      |      |      |
|      |      |      |      |     |      |      |      |       |      |      |      |
|      |      |      |      |     |      |      |      |       |      |      |      |

| Jan. | Feb. | Mar. | Apr. | May | June | July | Aug. | Sept. | Oct. | Nov. | Dec. |
|------|------|------|------|-----|------|------|------|-------|------|------|------|
|      |      |      |      |     |      |      |      |       |      |      |      |
|      |      |      |      |     |      |      |      |       |      |      |      |
|      |      |      |      |     |      |      |      |       |      |      |      |
|      |      |      |      |     |      |      |      |       |      |      |      |

# 9

## BRINGING THE FLOWER SEASONS
## INTO YOUR CHURCH

1. Basic Principles
2. Types of Containers
3. Arrangement Procedure
4. Suggested Arrangements for Various Seasons
5. Christmas
6. Easter
7. Memorial Day
8. June
9. Summer
10. Fall
11. Planning for Your Decorations

# BRINGING THE FLOWER SEASONS INTO
# YOUR CHURCH

In over 50,000 churches across the country floral decorations add to the beauty of the worship service each Sunday morning. In almost all of them some of the ladies of the church are called upon to arrange for these decorations as very few churches wish to spend the money for professional florist service. By the same token, the flowers also are furnished from the gardens of members of the church so that it is possible for the decorations to be in keeping with the season. It has been said of Dr. Theodore Parker of Boston that his pulpit "was a floral calendar from week to week, its wild roses, asters and gentians keeping step with the procession of the flowers across the valleys and hills."

There is much to consider in making really effective use of flowers and plants in the various types of churches which we have in this country. The architecture ranges from the lovely graceful New England Colonial with its light interior finished in white with brass accents through the traditional Cathedral with its dark and somber interiors and lofty reaches to the Modern Gothic which unites some of the light of the Colonial with the form of the Gothic into a delightful combination of light and formality.

## BASIC PRINCIPLES

For each of these types of architecture and their modifications, you will want to plan different kinds of floral decorations best suited to the individual backgrounds. In so doing, there are certain principles which you will want to follow:

1. In the church with a tall ceiling you will want to use the more formal types of flowers in your decorations. You will use masses of flowers, palms, everything in proportion to the size and height of the auditorium.

2. The smaller auditorium calls for less formal, lower bouquets. The flowers may even be those that you might use in your home, in larger masses, of course, but not the necessarily formal arrangements that are more appropriate in larger churches.

3. Be very careful in your use of color. Remember that purples and blues fade into a background of dark woods and hangings. Use contrasting colors such as white and red and yellows for the best effects. Although the use of much greenery is the custom, often it is not very effective and has become just a part of the background of a church which is taken for granted, adding very little to the real beauty of the sanctuary. The lovely pastels of "garden flowers" are particularly effective against the white of the Colonial churches although, with such a perfect background for floral settings as they present, you can almost let your imagination run rampant in the use of color.

## TYPES OF CONTAINERS

In nearly every church facilities have been provided in the way of containers for the floral arrangements. Very often these have been taken into consideration in the initial furnishing of the sanctuary in keeping with the setting of the chancel, pulpit, and altar. Large baskets or urns will be provided for placing bouquets in front of the pulpit and lectern, at the side of the organ, or in other appropriate places on the rostrum, while low, shallow containers will often be made use of on the altar, or communion table. I was in a church recently which was built in modern Gothic Style which had beautiful planters filled with tropical foliage enclosing the choir on either side of the rostrum in a very effective way.

Whatever is provided in the way of containers — and there may be several types which may be used at various times in your church — you will want to suit your arrangements to the container. Following are diagrams which will aid you in the ways of adapting your materials.

1. **Urn.** This type of container, most common in churches, adapts itself best to the circular arrangement. It is a massed arrangement and is made either with one flower in different sizes or with a variety of blooms. Light and shade are accomplished through proper placement toward the focal point or center of interest. The height of this arrangement is one and one-half times the length or width (whichever is the greater proportion). It very often adds to the design to show part of the rim of your container. This design is best made with 18 stems.

2. **Low bowl.** This is a twelve stem design which is very formal and would make a beautiful arrangement for the altar or communion table. There are practically unlimited combinations of flowers that can be used, ranging from roses, anemones, chrysanthemums and calla lilies, to combinations of delphinium and peonies, snapdragons and calendulas, larkspur and dahlias, buddleia and roses, etc. The basic thing to remember in this design is to keep the points of the triangle well-defined.

3. **Shallow container.** This is one of the loveliest of classic designs. It uses twelve stems and is particularly lovely in pairs on the altar with the long placements reaching toward the center. It is not as formal as the perfect triangle design, yet it is very effective and can make use of any of the flowers that you would use in the more formal arrangement. This design would also lend itself to use on pedestals placed on each side of the center pulpit.

4. **Oblong low container.** This arrangement is by far the easiest to do and can be done with a variety of flowers or foliage. One of the obvious good reasons for using this type of arrangement is that it takes very few flowers and can be used when flowers are at a premium.

While these designs are basic and may be of help to you, don't become tied to any set pattern. Use them only as a base and let your imagination have free rein. Your arrangements will be far more effective if you use your own creative ideas in the making of them.

## ARRANGEMENT PROCEDURE

After you have gathered the flowers which you are going to arrange for your church and have selected the containers best suited for the types of flowers that you have, there are a few things that you want to keep in mind having to do with their arrangement and care. We have listed them in order in the following paragraphs.

1. Harden the flowers. This is done by cutting the stems diagonally and plunging them in water up to their heads and allowing them to stand for several hours. When this is done the flowers stay fresh much longer.

2. When you have selected the containers, note their size, color, and contour, and the amount of water they will hold. This will enable you to decide how many flowers to use in your arrangement.

3. Use your light clear color on the outer edge and brighter deeper shades toward the lower and central part of the group.

4. Spike flowers such as snap dragons, stocks, dephiniums, larkspur, and lupin give height and will be above eye level. Round-faced flowers such as roses, peonies, carnations, etc., are better toward the center of the design. Part of the rim of the container should be allowed to show as it does much to complete the design.

5. In arranging your flowers, maintain the balance of the design by drawing an imaginary line down the center and being sure that the weight of the arrangement falls evenly on each side. Focus in arrangement is also important. It need not always be central, but it is the point to which your eye goes immediately and each arrangement needs a focal point. It is arranged by the use of the deepest color, the best flowers, or by an unusual shape.

6. Never overcrowd the flowers. Spread the stems so that they all appear to come from the same stalk, and make one color or one type of flower dominant in the design.

## SUGGESTED ARRANGEMENTS FOR VARIOUS SEASONS

The following are merely suggestions for arrangements for the various seasons of the year. These must be modified, of course, by the flowers which are numerous in your particular section of the country during the different seasons of the year. For instance, during the Christmas season if you live in Florida, you will use the Brazilian pepper berries which are so abundant in the woods in December; in California each yard is blooming with poinsettias of various types; and in Oregon the lovely traditional waxy-leafed English holly is to be found. With these thoughts in mind, we have merely made suggestios which you may find useful.

## CHRISTMAS

You will want to use the traditional Christmas decorations for your church. Somehow the more sophisticated modern combinations of color and plants for Christmas seem out of place in a church where the traditional Christmas story is the very essence of the season. We associate the red of the holly berries, the green of pine and cedar, and the stately crimson poinsettia with these traditions. Recently, we saw double poinsettias combined with calla lilies in a gorgeous display of color and texture in a bouquet. We would also suggest that greenery lighted with a single color of Christmas lights, preferably blue, gold, or white may be very beautiful in some churches.

## EASTER

Again you will want to use the traditional lilies and palm, but there are many possibilities at this season of the year in the use of spring flowers which make all kinds of delightful combinations. The lovely mingling of the pastel shades of sweet peas and stock with yellow roses; gladioli, narcissus, delphinium, lilies of the valley and violets. One of the very loveliest combinations for the Easter season is that of Easter lilies combined with heavenly blue delphinium. Branches in blossom are particularly beautiful for the chancel, bringing the very breath of spring and the flowering of the earth into the church, and low arrangements of hyacinths and narcissus are very effective for the altar and tables.

## MEMORIAL DAY

One of the most beautiful uses of flowers in the church of which we have ever heard was in the making of a service flag from flowers for a Memorial Day service. The flag was made of a piece of ¾" plywood 5¼' x 9', for the church was a very large one. It could have been 3½' x 6' just as well. The border was red peonies stuck through holes drilled in the background for the purpose. The center was the white background through which holes had been drilled for members of the families of service men to put either the deep blue iris or the gold ones as stars representing their men in the armed services. The gold iris, of course, were at the very center. The ceremony of which the floral display was the key was a very effective and beautiful one.

## JUNE

The center of your June and late spring decorations will, of course, be the roses that bloom so profusely during that time of the year. Various combinations of the roses themselves and roses with other flowers make very fine arrangements. They fit very well into stately, dignified arrangements as well as informal bouquets. In early June while lilacs are still in bloom they may very well be combined with almost any shade of roses. White roses and white stock make a cool and graceful bouquet. Low arrangements of red roses and lily of the valley, or yellow roses and lavender sweet peas are effective. Other flowers that are in the gardens at this season of the year and may be used very well are peonies, snapdragons, daisies, dahlias, asters, and larkspur.

## SUMMER

Make use of red poppies with blue and white delphinium for the early July services or larkspur and red roses and other red, white, and blue flowers to carry out the patriotic idea. Beautiful arrangements of bold colored zinnias are perfect for the summer season.

## FALL

The fall months are some of the best of the year to bring the lovely colors of the outside into the sanctuary. The beautiful golden shades of the harvest time are repeated over and over again in the chrysanthemums, golden rod, and red and gold leaves that abound at this time of the year. These leaves and flowers are particularly suited to floral decorations for church: the rich golden and winey hues fit in beautifully with the wood or stone interiors of most sanctuaries.

## PLANNING FOR YOUR DECORATIONS

Since the floral decorations of your church are an integral part of the setting for worship, we would suggest that space be allotted for the care and arrangement of flowers, containers, the necessary chicken wire needed to hold the arrangements in place and the floral clay which makes arranging so easy. When a new church building is being planned, it might very well be a good idea to plan a small room with cupboards and a sink with running water where the work with flowers could be done conveniently. In the older churches where no such room is available, certain cupboard space in the kitchen should be reserved for this purpose.

# 10

## CHURCH MEMBERS' BIRTHDAYS AND SPECIAL PROJECTS

1. Purposes of Funds
2. Beginning the Birthday Program
3. How to Follow Through
4. Letters Regarding Fund
5. Letter No. 1
6. Enclosure
7. Letter No. 2
8. Letter No. 3

# CHURCH MEMBERS' BIRTHDAYS AND
# SPECIAL PROJECTS

One of the most interesting plans for capitalizing upon birthdays is one which has been successfully used for a number of years in the Third Baptist Church of St. Louis. Third Church has something over eight thousand members and Dr. C. Oscar Johnson, the pastor, felt that it would be advisable for him to personalize in some way his very real interest in every one of his members.

Throughout the year, therefore, he sends to every member on his or her birthday a personal greeting card. Sometime after he started it, at the suggestion of several members who felt that on their birthdays they would like to remember one of the worthy causes in which Dr. Johnson was especially interested, there was added to the plan the idea that the recipients of such cards might respond by sending in an offering.

In Third Baptist Church it became a special scholarship fund. Everyone who received a card was given a cordial invitation to help build up such a fund for worthy young people, the fund to become a revolving one with no-interest loans made to young people so that they might attend college, to be paid back in later years.

It was an exceedingly popular cause and the fund has grown immensely during the years. There has never been any pressure upon anyone to make a gift of any particular size to it but the annual receipts have been exceedingly great. The fund has done a tremendous amount of good and all who have contributed to it have truly enjoyed the opportunity which Dr. Johnson has afforded them to participate in it.

## PURPOSES OF FUNDS

Any church which desired to use such a plan could well have in mind other special funds instead of the one which was selected by Dr. Johnson. There are several types of programs, however, for which it would be inadvisable. It would not be advisable, for instance, to have the minister send out a greeting card with an invitation to send money back which he would use for his own purposes, as, for instance, office expense, car allowance, etc. Such a cause would appeal to prospective donors as quite mercenary.

It would also not be advisable to use the fund for regular church expense. Funds for those purposes should be obtained through pledges and free-will offerings and not in this manner.

But a scholarship fund, almost any missionary activity, an organ or a building fund, since there can be no question of selfish interest on the part of the minister, are all worthy causes for such birthday offerings.

## BEGINNING THE BIRTHDAY PROGRAM

Most churches do not ordinarily have a record of the birth date of their members. Churches using membership application blanks usually have a place for such a statistic but most other churches do not. It is important, therefore, first of all, to get the birth date (the year is not important) of each member. This can easily be done by sending out a letter (Letter #1 at the close of this article is an example) to every member asking for this piece of information.

Since not everyone will respond it may be necessary to follow up the letter by a telephone call. There is no need to tell those who are called that the purpose of the information is to enable the minister to send out birthday greetings. The explanation could simply be made that the church office desires the information as a matter of record.

When the information has been received, it can be transcribed to a special birthday file set up on cards like the following:

```
                                                      Jan. 7


        Jones, John E.
        4828 Beaver Ave.




```

The cards would then be collated and arranged in the order of their dates. It would be well to get this information on every member before starting the program for if any member were missed he might feel hurt.

It might be a good idea to have a code letter for the general age group to which people belonged. If the church is large the minister would not remember the persons whose names he had on the roll, but "A" could represent ages from 8 to 15, "B" from 15 to 20, and "C" all above twenty and up to 60 or 70, with "D" representing aged parishioners. Such a division of the roll might help him to choose the type of card to send. Every few years, of course, these cards would have to be reclassified for age.

The ideal time to begin the program would be on the first of January since no one would have his feelings hurt if he had been missed in December.

## HOW TO FOLLOW THROUGH

It would be well in every instance to have the minister himself address the envelopes and sign his own name to the greetings. The church can make up a special greeting card if it so desired, but it should be changed annually, of course, and there are so many excellent birthday greeting cards on the market that it would be more economical to buy them than to make up its own.

Dr. Johnson had frequent out-of-town speaking engagements and he always took with him all of the cards needed to take care of the birthdays which would cover the period when he would be away. When he was absent at Antwerp during the meetings of the World Council of Churches he tried to time the greetings so that they would arrive on the birthday date. His people, therefore, knew that he was actually thinking of them while he was away and that this was not just a routine greeting which was sent out by the church office.

Whenever this plan is adopted it should be adopted on that basis. If the minister is to be gone for a few weeks he should plan to mail those greetings from the place where he is staying. If he is on vacation the greetings should be sent from the vacation spot. True, the cards can be prepared beforehand and bundled into separate daily releases but they should be sent from the place where the pastor is staying and not from the church.

It is also advisable to have an occasional accounting of the fund in the church bulletin or the church paper. Names of donors should never be given but should be a matter of record in official books. The pastor can have the checks made out to him for the psychological effect which such a procedure might have but he could also have some person in the church, perhaps the church treasurer, designated as the official custodian of the fund. It is always important to have such a record so that there can never be a breath of suspicion that the minister could be cashing and using checks for his own purposes.

## LETTERS REGARDING FUND

We are adding herewith two letters: Letter #2 which would be used to inaugurate the fund, and; letter #3 which could go at the beginning of the second year. Another letter would be sent out each succeeding year. It is always preferable to have the letters multigraphed with a space left for the insertion of the name of the person above the salutation. A good typist can be depended upon to have the letter look as if it had been freshly typewritten.

The date, the name and address of the person, and the salutation would be left off of the multigraphing job and inserted later as required. Since the same letter would go to new members received during the year it would be advisable to make up a considerable number of additional copies to take care of new members.

It should also be the duty of the church secretary to go over the file daily to remove the names of people who have transferred their memberships to other churches or people who have died. Unless this is done it is possible that embarrassing situations might ensue.

It is definitely preferable not to include a return envelope. To do so would give the entire procedure the air of being just another "stunt" for raising money. People who are interested in contributing to the fund would be enough concerned to address and stamp their own envelopes and include checks in them.

**LETTER #1**

## PROSPECT STREET METHODIST CHURCH

Twelfth and Prospect
San Francisco 4, Calif.

June 4, 1955

Mr. John E. Jones
4828 Beaver Avenue
San Francisco 12, Calif.

Dear Mr. Jones:

    In an effort to get as complete a file as is possible on every one of our fine members we are planning to include as one of the essential items on the personal cards in our files, the birth dates of all of our people.

    We would, therefore, appreciate it if you would fill in the birth dates on the cards which we enclose for you and the members of your family.

    We are not interested in securing the date of birth—which, as clerks at marriage license bureaus have occasionally discovered, is sometimes a query loaded with dynamite—but merely the date on which the birthday anniversary falls.

    Would you be so kind as to send these cards in at once in the enclosed, stamped envelope?

    Thanking you for this favor, I am

Cordially yours,

Marjory Williams,
Church Secretary

**ENCLOSURE**

Jones, John E.
4828 Beaver Ave.

Birthday _____    _____
                Month                Day

## LETTER #2

From the desk of:

Wilbur Youngman
Prospect Street Methodist Church
Twelfth and Prospect
San Francisco 4, Calif.

A time honored custom of many service clubs
on the occasion of a birthday or wedding anniversary
is to invite the person who has just celebrated
such an event to stand while the club sings
"Happy Birthday to You." The individual is then
invited to make a contribution to the youth work
or scholarship fund of the club—and he always
does so gladly.

We are inaugurating the same plan in our
church this year. In effect, I'm singing "Happy
Birthday to You." And in the quiet of my study
I'm lifting up a prayer for you and your other
fellow-members whose birthday falls on this day.
I am thanking the Lord for our friendship and
praying that health and long life may be yours.

And, if you feel that you would like to have
a part in the project, I'm inviting you to make
a special contribution today in honor of your
birthday to the work of our great missionary school
in Manamadura, India.

All of the money which is received for the
project will go to a scholarship fund which will
make it possible for students from the villages
near Manamadura to attend the school. Eight
dollars and fifty cents will support a student
for one month. Seventy-six dollars and fifty cents
will take care of a student for an entire year.

If you'd like to share in this project you're
invited to make your check payable to: James
Stoddard, Treasurer. Be sure to mark it "Scholarship Fund."

With best wishes for many happy years to come,
I am

Affectionately yours,

WY:jc

## LETTER #3

From the desk of:

> Wilbur Youngman
> Prospect Street Methodist Church
> Twelfth and Prospect
> San Francisco 4, Calif.

    Last year we started a custom which is well on its way to become a tradition. Instead of giving presents to our members who had birthdays, we offered them the opportunity to make gifts to one of the most interesting Christian projects that we knew—the granting of scholarships to young people in India to enable them to attend the Christian Institute at Manamadura.

    On December 31st we were happy to note that the members of our church, in response to those invitations, were able to offer full year scholarships to twenty-four outstanding young Indian students.

    Manamadura is an agricultural institute and our young students, when they graduate will go back to their own villages to help their people till their land more effectively, often quadrupling production. By our gifts, therefore, we will not only be spreading the Gospel of Jesus Christ but in a very practical way feeding the hungry, not for a brief period of time—for that often is merely temporary relief, but for years to come.

    I do want to thank you for the part that you played in this program even as I wish for you very many more happy birthdays, long life, and happiness. May God richly bless you as you come to another milestone in your eventful life.

Most sincerely yours,

P.S. Make checks payable to "James Stoddard, Scholarship Fund."

Note: On the preceding letters fill in the date of the person's birthday as the date of the letter, his name, address, and the salutation. Wherever possible make the salutation personal. Instead of "Dear Mr. Jones," write, "My dear John," or "My dear Jack." If possible sign the letters in the same way. Instead of the signature, "Wilbur Youngman," sign it "Wilbur" or "Bill" or by whatever nickname you use.

# 11

## HOW TO SERVE A CHURCH DINNER SPEEDILY AND EASILY

1. Organization Necessary
2. Setting the Tables
3. Salad and Bread
4. Waiting on Tables
5. From the Kitchen End

# HOW TO SERVE A CHURCH DINNER
## SPEEDILY AND EASILY

### ORGANIZATION NECESSARY

Many church kitchens are so poorly arranged that it is difficult both to prepare a meal in them and to serve a meal from them. The designers of church kitchens some years ago—differing from the modern designers who have done a most effective job—did not seem to realize that a church kitchen was altogether different from a home kitchen but also differed considerably from the kitchen in a restaurant or a hotel.

For churches interested in planning new kitchens or in doing over old kitchens we are now preparing a pamphlet with suggested plans after consultation with a great many experts in the field.

In this pamphlet, however, we want to start with your kitchen as it is now arranged to show you a better way to serve your meals, for this service can be speeded up considerably merely by properly arranging service both inside and outside of the kitchen. Basically it is the application of assembly line procedures to the situation which confronts a meals committee.

### SETTING THE TABLES

It is quite evident that the more things which can be put on the tables in the dining room the easier it is to serve a meal later on. We would suggest, therefore, that tables be set in this fashion:

(1) Use a roll of heavy white paper for your table cloth. Start it at one end of the table and roll to the other. Tear it off well beyond the end of the table. Get a stapling machine and fasten at each end and also along the sides with the stapler. Put in enough staples to anchor securely. After the meal is over you can pull off and burn the table cloth.

(2) In addition to decorations put all the silverware on the tables, plus sugar, cream, and condiments. Put your coffee cups and water glasses on the table and we would suggest that you set coffee and water pitchers on the table as well. It may be well to fill the glasses with cold water shortly before the meal but afterwards let the people at each table be on their own. If that is also done with the coffee pitchers, it will cut down the number of waiters needed or free them for other work.

One or two waiters can be assigned to keep the pitchers filled as needed. By planning for no more than two cups per person very little coffee will be wasted. We would suggest that after there has been a reasonable amount of service of coffee, the pitchers be taken up and one or two waitresses can then serve all the tables if some of the diners want extra cups.

## SALAD AND BREAD

It will also save considerable time if salads and bread are served from plates or bowls which are left right on the table. Since some people do not like gravy it would also be preferable to put gravy boats on the table to let people help themselves.

Despite the occasional jibes at cole slaw it is a salad that almost everyone enjoys and a tossed green salad is equally acceptable. When served out of a salad bowl it will not have the wilted look that church salads acquire when they are put on the table on individual plates too long before the dinner.

If jello salads are used they would have to be set out individually. They should be set out about twenty minutes before the meal is to be served so that they will not have time to melt and the lettuce leaves used as garnishes do not wilt. A little less water than the proportions suggested in recipes will make stiffer salads, but the amount of water reduction should be slight or the resultant gelatin may be leathery.

## WAITING ON TABLES

In many churches a great deal of time is wasted at the kitchen windows. Waiters crowd up to them to receive two plates each and, because others are crowding behind them, find it difficult to get away. Too much time is consumed in this way. Hence the need for careful planning of the route that waiters will use both going to and coming from the kitchen. We would suggest, therefore, that service be carried on in this fashion:

A. Always place the speaker's table farthest from the kitchen. ALL of the waiters will first serve this table, beginning at the near end as service is started. When this table has been served the waiters will move on to the next table farthest from the kitchen, then to the next, and so on.

When this plan is followed it will mean that all of the people at one table are ready for dessert at the same time. It will also save time if someone will be on hand to direct people to the tables before the dinner, seeing to it that each table is filled before the next one is used. Latecomers, therefore, will not occupy empty seats at partially filled tables but will all be seated together, can be served at the same time, and they will, of course, be nearest the kitchen.

When service is arranged in this way the dish-washing job will likewise be made easier since places which have been unoccupied can have their dishes collected separately and put back into cupboards without washing.

B. Have waiter traffic move counter-clockwise in all serving and when removing plates. This will keep traffic flowing always in the same direction and will keep waiters from bumping into one another. No matter which tables in a dining-hall are being served the out-going waiters would move along the right wall of the dining-hall, using the kitchen as the base of operations, and would return along the left wall to the kitchen for their new supplies.

The following diagram shows a typical church dining hall and indicates the waiter flow of traffic.

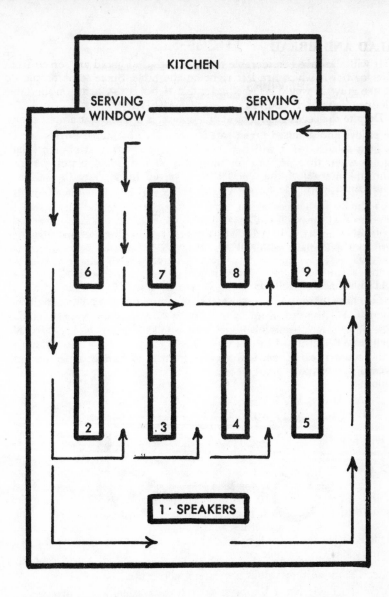

Table numbers indicate the sequence in which tables should be filled with diners and served. The single exception, of course, is the speakers' table. While it should be served first of all it is occupied by those who have been designated to sit there.

C. Build a service shelf just outside the serving windows in the kitchen. This can be hinged and let down when not in use but it makes service that much easier. We are illustrating it herewith:

D. Leave as much space as possible near the windows which are between the kitchen and the dining room. This helps to expedite the steady flow of waiters.

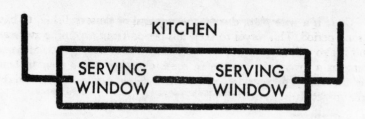

KITCHEN

SERVING
WINDOW

SERVING
WINDOW

E. When all of the diners have received their plates the waiters can give attention to the coffee and water pitchers, refilling whenever necessary.

F. After all of the diners at Tables No. 1 and 2 have finished with their dinners the waiters can begin to remove their plates. If the dining room is sufficiently large so that the aisles between tables can accommodate a cart the most effective way to handle this is to build a vehicle of this kind using dolly wheels, if possible, for the purpose. Lacking dolly wheels, good sturdy wheels from a boy's wagon will serve instead. The cart should have an upper and lower deck. It will save space if all of the dinner and salad plates are set on the upper deck and the salad bowls, and whatever else is to be collected at the time are set below.

The cart can be designed in this fashion. A handle at either end would be optional.

The cart illustrated above, of course, has wagon wheels. If dolly wheels are used they would not extend above the lower shelf.

When Table No. 2 has been cleared the waiters would proceed to Tables 3, 4, 5, 6, 7, and 8 in that order. They would be ready, as soon as they had finished, to serve dessert to Tables 1, 2, 3, and so on. Occasionally, it is wise to divide the waiters into two sections for this operation. One section would clear the tables and the other section would immediately follow them up and serve dessert.

It would be advisable then to serve coffee once more and take the coffee pitchers off the tables.

When the dinner dishes have been removed the waiters can proceed with the removing of the dessert dishes from Tables 1, 2, 3, 4, etc.

G. It is a wise plan, during the removal of dessert dishes, to have a song period. This serves to keep this period from becoming awkward and it also will keep people at the tables. Unless they are doing something as a group the custom in some churches is for men to leave the tables and go outside for a smoke. Often it takes a considerable time to get them back into place again.

## FROM THE KITCHEN END

Sometimes dinners go off very slowly because of the slowness with which service is carried on in the kitchen. It goes without saying, of course, that the meal should be altogether ready to serve by the time for which it is announced. In order to accomplish this it is wise to start the meal so early that it is actually ready a half hour before the time for which it has been set. No matter what foods are served this can be accomplished without any difficulty and the food kept hot whether or not the church uses steam tables. Steam tables are a tremendous boon, to be sure, but they are not essential except, probably, for the larger churches.

When it is time to serve an assembly line should be formed in the kitchen in the same way that it is formed among the waiters. If this is done a large company of people can be served in a matter of minutes. The basic pattern for an assembly line for the kitchen would consist of: the food to be served, ready in such quantities that there would be no need to stop for additional supplies; stacks of plates; a line of servers; and sufficient room for organization.

Pick your people for these spots. If you have people working in the kitchen who are very slow don't put them on a serving line for they will hold up the line. As many serving lines can be organized as are needed but each would consist basically of the following arrangements:

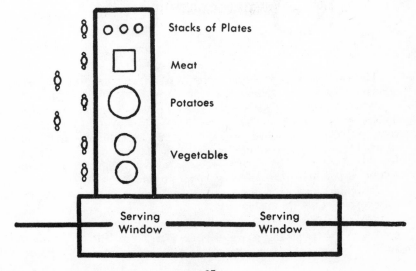

We have used the following as the symbol for a server: oOo The server at the end of the table would pick up a plate, hand to the meat server, who in turn hands it to the potato server, then to the vegetable server, who hands it to the person on the end who pushes it out through the window to one of the waiters. If gravy is added there would be one other person in the line, of course, for no one person should serve two different items on one plate.

We have in reserve two people who will be ready to bring additional platters of meat, potatoes, or vegetables as needed. The same arrangement can be made for the other serving window and, if desired, there can be lines of servers on both sides of a single table.

Where steam tables are used the servers would get their supplies right from them if they are located in close proximity to the serving window. The plan which we have outlined will make possible the service of the maximum number of people in the minimum amount of time and will do away with unnecessary milling about in the kitchen.

As soon as the main course has been completed the tables can be set up with dessert. If ice cream is served it is advisable to use a scoop to dip out of gallon cartons or to get individual servings. Don't let the ice cream freeze too solid. If the cartons are packed with dry ice remove it about an hour before the dinner and store in a cool place to allow it to soften.

The serving windows should not be used to receive the soiled dishes. They should be brought into the kitchen by another route, possibly through a door, and stacked in a location as near to the spot where they are being washed as possible but at some distance from the serving area.

# 12

## HOW TO COSTUME BIBLICAL PLAYS INEXPENSIVELY

1. Obtaining Materials
2. New Testament Characters
3. Women
4. Romans
5. Angels

# HOW TO COSTUME BIBLICAL PLAYS EFFECTIVELY AND INEXPENSIVELY

It is not our purpose in the following pages to create elaborate designs for various costumes or to make use of difficult and expensive materials, but rather to show you how to costume Biblical plays easily and effectively with materials which may already be at hand or which may be purchased very inexpensively. Instead of going into detail as to the authenticity of various details of costume, it will be our purpose merely to make each nation and period distinguishable from the other and indicate social rank especially in the time of Christ.

## OBTAINING MATERIALS

Remnant counters in stores where textiles are available will be your most valuable source of costuming materials. Bright hued materials of various textures and shades will be indispensable for turbans, tarbushes, girdles, sashes, etc. Look particularly for goodly lengths of striped materials and pieces with deep indigos, purples and brilliant yellows predominating. Plain ugly browns simulating rough handwoven materials and many yards of cheap unbleached muslin are useful. Veils can be made from curtain muslin in pale colors. Any remnants of buckram and tailor's canvas will come in very handy as well as pieces of bright colored canvas.

End-of-the-season sales at which sandals are sold will take care of the need for barefoot type sandals which were worn almost exclusively during Bible times. Additional lengths of thongs or tapes can be added to the sandals to simulate the lacings that were worn to the knee by the Roman soldiers of the day.

"Junk" jewelry counters will fill the need for the rich jewels that were worn by the wealthy people of the time. Heavy rings and bracelets that were worn by the women often have their counterparts on the jewelry counters in dime stores. Big glass pins will fill the need for decorations on the turbans of the Kings of the Orient. Strings of bright colored beads and heavy earrings of the dangling type will be in demand for your costumes.

Textile paints will be invaluable in stenciling borders on materials to simulate embroidery. Designs of all kinds will make the costumes more elaborate and will distinguish the rich, ornate dresses of the rich from the plain, simple costumes of the poor. Avoid the use of black except to designate mourning for which it was always used.

## NEW TESTAMENT CHARACTERS

Jews.

1. Townsmen — scribes, merchants, religious teachers, etc.
   a. Overdress in striped material, either cotton or silk. Slit at sleeve to allow the underdress to show through.
   b. Off white cotton underdress either full length to show at the neck, sleeve, and ankle, or merely strips of the white material sewed on at these points to simulate an undergarment.

c. Bright girdle made of a scarf or bright piece of cretonne.

d. Turban and tarbush of plain or heavy striped cotton for the poor; thin pale material for the wealthier class.

2. Villagers—farmers, fishermen, carpenters, etc. Probably the costume of Jesus and his disciples.

a. White underdress reaching halfway between knee and ankle with sleeves to wrist. Unbleached sheeting.

b. Girdle of heavy leather or canvas webbing.

c. Thick coat of goats' or camel hair striped dark brown and white in varying widths. It can be simulated by sewing white unbleached stripes on dark brown canvas. Made by two lengths of material, about 26 inches wide, laid side by side and joined with a rough seam. Embroidery around the neck can be indicated with textile paint.

d. Turban or a bright cotton square about 49 x 49 inches with one corner turned in to make an uneven triangle and kept in place with a horsehair coil. This coil may be made by using a black sateen tube stuffed with wadding.

3. Shepherds will wear this costume with an undressed sheepskin added, worn either with the fur or leather side out. Also to their dress will be added the weapons necessary to their trade.

a. Rod—club about 2 ft. long, the heavy end studded with nails hanging from a leather thong looped about the wrist.

b. Staff—an uneven crook cut from a tree may be made from wire and padded.

c. Sling—carried hanging from the belt. The belt is crocheted or braided from cotton of bright colors.

4. Boys or very young men wear the same costume as their elders except that they use a cap which may be made from a stocking top fitted on the back of the head to one side.

5. *Bedouins* also wore the above costume except that the white under dress has long sleeves which are pointed on the lower side and the overdress was often all black. Also the headdress was always a bright square, sometimes made of silk with some shade of yellow generally predominating.

6. *High priests.*

a. Coat or robe of white material fitting to throat with a band and with tight sleeves. It extends to the ankles.

b. Girdle or long sash, about 4 inches broad, of soft thin material painted in designs of scarlet, purple and blue to simulate heavy embroidery. It is wound several times around the body and tied at the breast with long ends hanging down.

c. Overdress made of heavy blue cloth to simulate linen, and stenciled with bands of scarlet, purple and blue pomegranates alternating with golden bells. You might hang real bells on this garment to jingle at times and it may be made in two pieces, just fastened at the shoulders.

    d. Breastplate made of heavy cloth, such as canvas stenciled to look like embroidery and set with "precious stones". It is held in place by cords attached to the shoulders by jewels and fastened to the overdress by cords of blue just above the girdle.

    e. Headdress may be made by use of the crown of a hat heightened by adding a head band. Pad out the hat to hold it in shape, cover it with pale cream cotton material, and trim it with blue material and a gold knob on top.

7. Priests should wear the above costume except for the breastplate. However, it should be all white except for the girdle which is a different color from the girdle of the high priest.

8. *Temple Guards.*

    a. The underdress will be a light yellow of nondescript material reaching halfway between knee and ankle.

    b. The coat is made of rough brown material reaching about to the knees.

    c. Turban, fairly large and full, of pale yellow. It could match the underdress. Light muslin or cheese cloth with painted gold stripes for officers.

    d. Girdle—bright striped material—cretonnes or artificial silk will be fine.

## WOMEN

        Women fall into 3 main classifications as far as dress is concerned. The differences are sometimes minor but serve to distinguish characters and backgrounds on the stage.

1. Village women—probably worn by the Virgin Mary.

    a. The robe is deep blue reaching to the instep and open at the neck where it is decorated with a nine-inch square of embroidery (stenciling will be fine) in a design which is predominated by red. The seams of the robe are often decorated and the sleeves reach to the wrist with points falling to the calf of the leg.

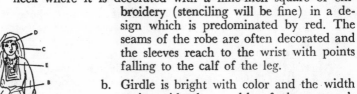

    b. Girdle is bright with color and the width varies with the wealth of the woman's husband.

    c. The veil for poor women was white and sheeting may be used very well for this purpose. Rich women wore veils of thinner material which may have had some embroidery on them.

d. Caps, worn under the veil, were made from a piece of red material about 11 x 18 inches. Tapes at the four corners of the square tied the hair back. Thin gold coins were stitched across the front and hung down on the forehead to denote wealth of husband. These coins may be made from painted cardboard.

e. Jewelry—strings of beads, anklets, rings, and charm earrings were the most common type of jewelry.

2. Nazareth women.

   a. Trousers—loose and of thin printed cotton material.

   b. Deep colored coat fitted at top with long tight sleeves, skirt of the coat flared out. Neck and sleeves ornamented at neck and wrists. This may be easily done with paint.

   c. Girdle is of a soft figured material about 2 yds. long by ¾ yds. wide.

   d. Veil of cheap curtain muslin, worn over cap with coins.

3. Bethlehem women.

   a. Long robe made of material which has multi-colored stripes.

   b. Girdle of mixed colors in a soft dull effect to blend rather than contrast with the brilliant hues of the robe.

   c. Hat for married women is brillantly decorated fez-shaped, covered with coins and string to tie under the chin.

   d. Veil is embroidered unbleached cloth fringed with bright colors. It is worn over the hat by married women, while the unmarried women and girls wear the veil without the hat.

# ROMANS

1. Citizen of Rome.

   a. Tunic—reaching to just above the knee and bloused over a narrow belt. It may be made from unbleached sheeting with striped or purple stuff from shoulder to hem back and front, on the tunics of the patrician class. The ordinary citizen wore the same tunic with no distinguishing stripes.

   b. Toga—length of material fitted to the height of the wearer and made from the same material as the tunic. It too will be striped with bands of purple in the case of the patrician.

c. Laced boots or leggings may be made of heavy material attached to sandals and laced up the front.

2. Roman soldier.

    a. Tunic may be either of a strong color or of unbleached muslin as above. The heavier the material the better in this case as it will hang better under the coat of mail.

    b. Coat of mail may be made from dish cloths which have been dyed dark brown and silvered a little. The tabs which are attached to fall over the shoulder and from the bottom may be made of canvas or felt to simulate leather.

## ANGELS

The costuming of angels is best accomplished by making simple long robes of white or pale yellow (depending on the lights you are using on the stage). The material should be quite thin so that it will have a soft downy effect on the stage.